Taking Charge

TAKING CHARGE

On Responsibility and Personal Identity

Manuel Cruz

Translated by Richard Jacques

continuum

2011

Continuum International Publishing Group
80 Maiden Lane, New York, NY 10038
The Tower Building, 11 York Road, London SE1 7NX

www.continuumbooks.com

Library of Congress Cataloging-in-Publication Data
Cruz, Manuel, 1951–
[Hacerse cargo. English]
Taking charge: on responsibility and personal identity / Manuel Cruz; translated by Richard Jacques.
     p. cm.
ISBN 978-1-4411-4775-2 (hardback: alk. paper)
ISBN 978-1-4411-4739-4 (paperback.: alk. paper) 1. Responsibility—Political aspects. I. Title.

JA79.C78913 2011
158.2—dc22   2011005239

ISBN: 978-1-4411-4739-4 (PB)
          978-1-4411-4775-2 (HB)

Typeset by Pindar NZ, Auckland, New Zealand
Printed and bound in the United States of America

Contents

Foreword by Gianni Vattimo — vii

Preface — xii

Introduction — 1

Chapter 1 The Problem that Concerns Us: Responsibility and Identity — 15

Chapter 2 Toward an Innocent Responsibility — 33

Chapter 3 Nostalgia for the Horizon — 59

Chapter 4 An Opportunity for a Different Identity (More on Tolerance) — 69

Epilogue: The Insomniac's Meditation — 103

Index — 121

Foreword

I can begin by saying that this book by Manuel Cruz, which is now finally available in Italian, is an excellent example of the "ontology of the present." However, I do not know if the author will consider this a compliment, since it is more a way of trying to associate his work with a philosophical project he may not share, despite our ties of friendship. So let me say just this: Cruz's book, like few others I have read this year (one of them, in the field of philosophical narrative, is certainly Umberto Eco's *Foucault's Pendulum*), is a text I would like to have written myself. I would just clarify, for the many readers who quite legitimately do not understand the term, what I mean by "ontology of the present." I take the expression from Michel Foucault, who in one of his essays proposed a distinction between two kinds of philosophy: an "analytics of truth," which engages in the study of the traditional questions of knowledge (science, logic etc.), and an "ontology of the present." The latter is an expression that, I am not sure to what extent being faithful to Foucault, I use in a Heideggerian spirit to say that since metaphysics (the theory of being as being, of the stable and universal foundations of all entities) is finished, what philosophy can and must do is try to grasp the meaning of being in its present configuration, since being is not a stable structure (it will thus be reduced to an object, while it is the condition of any objective possibility occurring); it is history, the history of the configurations, or "openings" as Heidegger says, in which it gradually occurs.

But enough autobiography. It was only to state my admiration for, and harmony with, Cruz's work, whatever the difference of emphasis behind our basic positions. Although at the beginning — I say this for readers with a more strictly "continental" training — the text seems mostly interested in a rather detailed description of the term "responsibility," as we read on we realize that at the heart of his analysis there are far vaster problems than the usual ones of analytic philosophy (or at least of the caricature of it we continentals often adopt to stir up controversy). We are reminded of (even if not explicitly referred to) problems similar to the ones we remember having found in the Sartre of the *Critique of Dialectical Reason*, or (though here the references are more specific) the Gadamer of *Truth and Method*; and perhaps to the Heidegger of *Being and Time*; the question of individual responsibility in our globalized communication and easy exchange mass society and, in different terms that Cruz has opportunely reviewed, the question of the hermeneutic circle or the authenticity of Heidegger's theorized existence, or the problem of alienation and the meaning of history that Sartre talks about. As you will remember, in the "Question of Method," which is the introduction to the *Critique of Dialectical Reason*, Sartre proposes the thesis that the alienation Marx speaks of must be read as the impossibility for the individual to understand and control the effects of his actions. In capitalist society, in which the product of labor is taken from the producers to become the capitalist's profit, all individual actions, including those not directly "productive" of goods, take on a significance that the agent is not aware of and cannot control. The social order of capitalist domination expropriates the whole historical meaning of what he does, uses it for purposes that remain unknown and strange to the actor, just as the global meaning of what he is doing escapes the operator on the production line, in the framework of the division between manual labor and managerial tasks, and so forth. For Sartre that expropriation can only end when, in revolutionary action, the individual identifies himself with the "group-in-fusion" and finally appropriates, along with other things, the meaning of history at the very moment he does so. The trouble is that when the revolution is over, by a sort of principle of inertia, the unifying heat of the group tends to burn out: the hierarchy is reestablished and the division of labor returns, and so alienation does too. Sartre's *Critique of Dialectical Reason* appeared at the beginning of the 1960s and seems like a synthesis of the revolutionary hopes of that decade and their defeat. It is in the climate of that "failure" (we cannot deny that for many people it was a sort of return to sanity) that we are still living today, and therefore also the reason the issues Cruz discusses in this book are current and urgent. In the meantime, the reasons for what to Sartre seemed a desperate relapse into alienation have revealed themselves with increasing clarity; at least in the sense that the mass society, developing toward the present condition of a thrusting globalization, makes the division between what we know about the meaning of our actions and their effective scope in the overall picture ever more dramatic. Not only that: more or less paradoxically, what Cruz calls "nostalgia for the horizon" has been heightened enormously, whereas our power of intervention in what happens seems to have shrunk — at least in proportion to the amount of information we are supplied with. We might think that, in the conditions of information "in real time" we live in (and despite the manipulation the news is subjected to by a wide range of interests), we citizens of the new millennium must be in ideal conditions to identify the immediate and the "general" meaning of our actions. On the other hand, we know very well that our very alienation from them increases our neurosis: the use of tranquilizers is spiraling every year and not only through the fault of advertising by the pharmaceutical companies. It is an imbalance similar to the one biologists have pointed out behind the predictive capacity of diagnostic medicine and its therapeutic capacity: you can know that there is every possibility of developing a cancer in the next few years but you do not know how to prevent it.

Obviously, in light of that, Cruz's discussion recalls so many other subjects of the philosophy of the last two centuries, beginning with the Nietzsche of the second of his *Untimely Meditations*, the one "On the Use and Abuse of History for Life." In it he had already described contemporary man as sick with the "illness of history," a kind of indigestion of the notions of his past and his current world that cannot be truly digested and so weigh on the stomach, foiling any initiative. The excess of "historiography" kills the capacity to make history.

In many ways that sickness is ours too, that of "democratic" societies, in which we wonder with increasing frequency if there is really anything to be said about collective life. The so-called crisis of the parties, an easily recognizable version of the relapse into the "inert practice" Sartre spoke about, is just one aspect of the general "neutralization" through which we all feel responsible (for the AIDS epidemic in Africa, for "hunger in the world," for environmental degradation, etc), but we soon quiet our conscience with one of many symbolic initiatives, such as the classic rock concert, the profits of which go to any of the good causes popularized by the media . . . In that framework, what Cruz observes about responsibility by omission is decisive. And sins of omission may be the most frequent and difficult to recognize, and the expression "taking charge" which gives the book its title is highly appropriate to indicate the "virtue" that should save us from that sin.

Even in our philosophy, complex reasons militate against a frank and decided affirmation of the taking charge that Cruz discusses, and we must admit to not having thought about it sufficiently. First of all, the diffidence about the emphasis placed on the subject and his decisions, an emphasis that seems quite disproportionate to the "medianess" in which our existence takes place. If in traditional societies everything developed according to custom, and rarely did anyone, at great risk, question that custom and common prejudices (except for sinning, naturally, often "fortiter," feeling remorse and tranquilizing oneself with confession or, worse still, with the purchase of an indulgence), today what Heidegger called the world of "man," of "speak, do, die," of everyday falsity, has so expanded its boundaries that it is becoming more and more difficult not to be a conformist. Young people no longer have the traditional possibility of abandoning the church for the path of sexual liberation, and the confessors have become extremely indulgent . . .; but even the most traditionally stigmatized "vices," such as homosexuality, have become "lifestyles," widely accepted, and most of all cultivated by the economy as niches of potential profit. Should we lament that liberalization? Of course not, not even Cruz proposes that; he merely expresses with clarity and decision (the word is appropriate here) his discomfort at the side effects of all that on the meaning of our lives, collective and even individual. Nietzsche rightly warned, in the notes to his "The European Nihilism" of the summer of 1887, that in the world of complete nihilism — but we can say: of the media neutralization of any difference — if one does not become an *Übermensch*, a "superman" (one capable of interpreting himself), one perishes. The ways out Cruz proposes are only apparently far from that Nietzschean imperative; they can be read as by no means banal developments of the premises presented by the great classics of authenticity, from Nietzsche to Heidegger, enriched by an attention unaffected by the analytic tradition. The insistence of many masters of contemporary philosophy on meeting and listening to the other — we think most of all of Lévinas, but also of Gadamer's or Ricoeur's hermeneutics, or Habermas's communication action or Benjamin's "messianism without a messiah" and then Derrida — which in Cruz has become a specific proposal for rereading tolerance in terms of knowledge. Tolerance, a term rightly suspected for its paternalistic implications, can become "a gnoseological virtue, a way of reaching the *I*, because with knowledge of the other we know ourselves in our specific historicity as well." The motto of Greek wisdom can still be the guide of the man of "globalized civilization."

Gianni Vattimo

Preface

This book was written bit by bit, in short bursts. I would not want anyone to think that I am making a virtue of necessity, but the truth is that that procedure allowed me to enjoy the rare privilege of submitting the ideas I finally put together here to a sustained examination. The rareness of the privilege does not allude solely to the proverbial absence of criticism in our community of philosophers — always more inclined to silence than debate — but to the quality of the interlocutors. I have had the opportunity to present the first drafts of this book at different forums and in various publications. And it was what we might call the *critical benevolence* of the successive readers and listeners that finally led me to publish it.

I shall try to the best of my ability not to make these first pages an endless list of people, congresses and specialized journals, which would sorely try the reader's patience, though I must admit that the list of acknowledgments is a very long one. I have begun this preface by warning that, not only because to my way of thinking transparency is the author's elementary obligation to the reader (whose anger when what he was presented with as new turns out to be familiar is fully justified), but also because certain contextual references to the origin of the works and the interlocutors who put forward objections and suggestions — that is, from the particular *companies* of each one — can often help the reader to compose a more complete image of the scope of the theoretical framework in which the idea is being presented.

Various drafts of the first chapter were presented at the International Colloquium "Spinoza: teología, ética y política," held in Santiago de Chile in May 1995, and the Philosophy Congress "¿Para qué Filosofía?" held in Granada in September 1995. I also had an opportunity to discuss some of the arguments in the cycle "O destino dos valores ó final do milenio," which took place at Fundación Paideia, La Coruña, in March 1996. There is a version, which does not coincide with the one that appears here, as an introduction to Hannah Arendt, *Entre historia y acción*, published by Paidós, and another, different again, in Italian ("Il dibattito che ci coinvolge: soggeto e responsabilità," *Iride* 21, Year X, August 1997, Florence).

The ideas for the second chapter ("Toward an Innocent Responsibility") were first discussed at the colloquium "Problemas de universalismo y contextualismo," held at the Universidad Veracruzana, Jalapa, Veracruz (Mexico), in May 1996, as a result of a happy initiative of Mariflor Aguilar. As the work grew I could compare its development in other spheres: as part of the conference "¿De qué se habla cuando nos referimos a la discapacidad?" held at Fundación Paideia, La Coruña, in February 1997, at the international symposium "La reflexión histórica en las disciplinas humanas y en las prácticas sociales," held at the Humanities Faculty of the Universidad Nacional del Comahue, Neuquén (Argentina), in October 1997, organized by María Inés Mudrovcic, or in the cycle on the subject of responsibility organized jointly by the chair of contemporary philosophy at the Universidad de Barcelona and the CSIC Institute of Philosophy, to which I shall refer later. Part of what appears here was published in the journal *Isegoría*, no. 17 November 1997, under the title "Conviene cambiar de figuras. Sobre acción y responsabilidad." Shortly afterward an expanded version appeared in Italian, from where the definitive title comes: "Verso una responsabilitá innocente," *Filosofia Politica*, Year XII, no. 2, August 1998, Bologna.

A first draft of the third chapter, "Nostalgia for the Horizon," was read at the conference "Jornadas sobre individuo y subjetividad," held in Jalapa, Veracruz (Mexico), in May 1997 and, a few months later, at the IX Congreso Nacional de Filosofía, organized by the Asociación Filosófica de la República Argentina and held in La Plata (Argentina) in October 1997.

The ideas for the fourth chapter were basically discussed at two forums. The first was the cycle "Concepciones y narrativas del yo," organized by the philosophy department of the Faculty of Philosophy and Letters Faculty (Universidad de Málaga) in April 1997. The second, the colloquium entitled "Fraternitá, ostilitá, comunitá," organized by the philosophy department of the Università degli Studi di Salerno, the philosophy and politics department of the Istituto Universitario Orientale di Napoli, and the Istituto Italiano per gli Studi Filosofici, in Naples, in May 1998. Useful elements were also provided by the debate at the Third International Workshop "Paradigmas

Emancipatorios. Balance y Perspectivas de Fin de Siglo," in Havana in January 1999. Part of the work is included in M. Cruz (comp.), *Tolerancia o barbarie* (Barcelona: Gedisa, 1998).

Lastly, the Epilogue, "The Insomniac's Meditation," was the text of the inaugural lecture of the Cátedra Libre de Estudios Hispánicos "Maria Zambrano," organized by the Spanish Embassy and the Philosophy Faculty of the University of Buenos Aires in September 1997. It was published in the journal *Debats*, no. 57/58, Autumn–Winter 1996.

In addition to all those activities I cannot omit the mention of two other initiatives that enabled me to put many of the theses presented here to the test. One was the cycle "Individualismo e responsabilitá," held at the Istituto Italiano di Cultura de Barcelona in April 1996, and the other, the conference on the subject of responsibility and personal identity in modernity that, with the same title as this volume, was held in Barcelona and Madrid in December 1997 and January 1998. This second initiative was the result of a collaboration, which can only be described as happy and profitable, with the research group coordinated by Roberto Rodríguez Aramayo, of the CSIC Institute of Philosophy, a collaboration that in administrative language is called, somewhat reiteratively, Unidad Asociada. I must also express my thanks — not solely for obvious theoretical reasons but also for personal ones — for the observations that, with the healthy ferocity that is their salient feature, were made to me by Ernesto Garzón Valdés, Reyes Mate, Javier Muguerza, Concha Roldán, Carlos Thiebaut, Antonio Valdecantos and José Luís Villacañas, as well as the coordinator himself.

I am aware that the list is starting to be excessively long (although I have tried to keep it short), but since economy can never be used as an alibi for ingratitude, I have left for the end a mention that is particularly important to me on different levels. Antonio Aguilera, Fina Birulés, Santiago López Petit, Román Gutiérrez Cuartango, Julieta Piastro, Marina Garcés, Laura Llevadot, not forgetting Carmen Corral in the first stage of the team's life, have been far more than an administrative unit for my work in the last few years. I could confine myself to saying that they read the text with generous attention as it was taking shape and made some valuable comments — the spirit of which I hope I have been able to capture — but that would fall short of the truth. They have been a true research group — of which I am proud to have been a member — but also a discussion group; a small, warm, living community who provided me at every step, with rare intuition, with the dose of calm and enthusiasm, support and censure, necessary to guarantee the continuity of the work. Together or separately, their suggestions, their observations and even their silences have been a permanent reference point, a tutelary criterion, for me at all times. I would like to think I have made good use of it and in any case I can only express my gratitude to them.

Perhaps most of the people mentioned will not recognize the final text they gave their opinions on at the time, owing to the number of changes I have felt obliged and delighted to introduce thanks to their contributions. It is true that little remains of the first drafts. But I prefer not to draw the obvious conclusion that any mistakes that might remain after so much sifting are all mine; I would rather emphasize that the final text is in many ways a collective work. A collective of friends, if you like, but friends who are that thanks to their intelligence and passion for philosophy, which is a reason for added satisfaction for this author, who has benefited from both.

Manuel Cruz

Introduction

Philosophers have a tendency to give articles, books or chapters titles like "the return of the concept of . . .", "toward a new notion of . . ." and so on. Titles of which the purpose is to arouse in the reader a slightly dizzy feeling of being an eyewitness to a transcendental moment in the history of thought, or perhaps to insinuate, without giving it too much importance, that what he is witnessing is not a simple change but a complete break with the past, not to say a revolution in theory or perhaps even a leap into the abyss of thought itself.

However, the sum of our experience should make us more prone to caution. There is often something deceptive about such phrases. In this venerable activity, no idea resigns itself to being definitively retired. They are all, in a certain sense, always on active service, although that activity may be frankly languid or even merely residual. In fact, above and beyond their exaggeration, what those expressions indicate is a change of direction, a shift of emphasis or a variation in perspective that, with time, may enlighten a different way of thinking. But in their present, things are always confused and, at the moment they appear, what will later be called tendencies, conceptual revolutions or any other terms from the usual historiographical toolkit, will hardly amount to anything more than an excessive becoming, a disordered course of events to be interpreted.

In recent times the idea of responsibility seems to have recovered a certain theoretical attraction in intellectual spheres that, until a short while ago, were resistant to it. Various factors of different natures (sometimes decidedly extraphilosophical) have contributed to this. It is not yet the moment to embark on an analysis of the reasons for either the attraction or the rejection, but perhaps it is the moment to note that change and try to insert it into a provisional framework of meaning. The aim is to inform the reader of something of this from the beginning; in the case of a book, it is always the title. As I understand it, the expression "take charge" has the virtue of supplying that initial indication, of pointing out the path to be followed, the direction presumed to be the right one. Because the Spanish phrase for taking charge, *hacerse cargo*, is unambiguously an ambiguous expression, we can use it both to claim responsibility (what happens when we wonder, for example, who is going to pay for the damage caused by a particular action) and to ask for understanding (what happens when we ask someone else to put themselves in our place).

We shall observe that the ambiguity is greater or smaller according to the contexts. It might be argued that there is a context in which the ambiguity becomes so blurred that it no longer seems like ambiguity. With a person, the argument goes, we use the same expression in both contexts, because we are actually saying the same thing. We are demanding or asking — as the case may be — him to assume, or to make his own, a situation or an action. To put himself in our place for whatever is required, including both responding to possible demands and understanding our point of view.

Far from invalidating any hypothesis, the possible existence of a semantic territory where the uses are confused even strengthens some of the hypotheses underlying this text. The reader will notice that the subtitle includes another category, personal identity, which has a strong theoretical link with the previous ones. It has not been put in such a strategic place just to announce that the subject may be found as the book unfolds but, rather, to explain the almost indissoluble character of the categorical pair. If there are no people, there is no confusion (for example, it would make little sense — beyond a not very poetic anthropomorphization — for anyone to ask the administration to put itself in their place), but perhaps because there is no genuine responsibility — or, rather, the responsibility that matters most to us — in such uses.

Together with this theoretical determination, from its very utterance the title *Taking Charge* also seeks to focus attention on another, generally less emphasized, aspect of the question, an aspect we might well term gnoseological, or pertaining to knowledge. The matter is neither obvious nor trivially true. The persistent and widespread tendency to identify the subject of responsibility with a subject that belongs basically to the sphere of the discourse of ethics should undoubtedly be analyzed from the perspective of the history of ideas, and here it would not be difficult to find important motives for explaining the identification. But genealogy cannot exhaust the analysis or prevent us from recording other aspects of it.

For it may be that this permanent recourse to ethics is related to the fact that the ultimate origin of responsibility is found in notions linked to discourses of a fundamentally theological nature. And so such a fact may be a limitation at some moment, but in no way can it become a condemnation (which, to cap it all, would not admit redemption). In the end, almost all our notions have the same or a similar origin, and that has not prevented humanity from taking firm steps toward an immanent conception of the world. The question, therefore, should not be posed in terms of a previous ruling about a presumed epistemological *blood cleansing*, but of a consideration of the extent to which, beyond their variable origins, the notions we use have undergone a genuine process of secularization or, to put it another way, of emancipation from the guardianship of religion (I am thinking specifically of the analyses Giacomo Marramao has made throughout his work in relation to the unequivocally Judaeo-Christian origin of the ideas of freedom and equality, an origin that has not prevented, indeed has even encouraged, the emergence of an effectively secularized modernity).

That emancipation, we might say, is the kind that liberates the host of meanings of the category of responsibility, as is the case with the category of identity. The latter must also be examined as far as possible from the present, and an effort made for the weight of the past (for example, of certain impossible humanisms) not to blind us to a cluster of transformations that oblige us to reconsider some of its features. This general, initial affirmation — which will be dealt with in more detail on several occasions later — could be exemplified in the light of some of the subjects raised in the fourth chapter.

For, indeed, in the case of identity, the correlate of that danger of *moralizing* responsibility is the danger of essentializing it. And we should warn that that danger does not appear solely in the old guise of traditional, metaphysical, historical essentialism — the kind, for example, that enjoyed likening identity to the old, gross categories of traditional philosophical anthropology (Man, Person and a few others), all of which can be gathered under the idea they all spring from, the idea of the soul. Oddly enough, far from making them disappear, many of the criticisms leveled in recent years at any of those notions have made them multiply on another scale. In a certain sense — which needs to be qualified immediately so that surprise does not lead to misunderstanding — many of the processes that have gained the greatest ascendancy lately in advanced Western societies could be interpreted as reappearances — now much weakened and straitened, perhaps — of the old identities.

But reducing identity (even if in order to be able to make it plural) involves a not very radical theoretical attitude, for all it may be decked out in iconoclastic and provocative terminological garments. On the contrary, it rather implies remaining within the schema that is apparently the one to be criticized. Such would be the case of some of those discourses that, sometimes using the pretext of the defense of multiculturalism (or interculturalism, or whichever equivalent term may be regarded as the most suitable one at any given moment), or sometimes some other theoretical and political one, move hastily from a defense of the right to difference to a frankly ontologizing affirmation of the existence of someone different. Along the way there is an anthropomorphization, a reification of what in fact is no more than a feature, a determination or characteristic, but that, almost by the art of categorical magic, is turned into an essence that completely fills the content of the identity.

In recent years we have seen a generalization of a kind of discourse that appeals to age, gender, nationality, race, religion, sexual preference, if not to the habitual use of some substance, or even some particular circumstance (as when that reporter from an Argentine TV station asked a possible victim of the flooding of the Paraná River: "are you *one of the flooded*?") to defend the dubious condition of *different*. Perhaps the initial sympathy with which ideas of this kind were received at the time has to do with a ghost from our immediate past, the ghost of uniformization, of homogenization, typical of a developed capitalism, which seemed to threaten to crush all difference.

But obviously that hypothetical undesired effect of the ultimate evolution of our society does not mean that any reaction to it is good. It is frankly doubtful that the *proliferation of à la carte identities* is a suitable response to the dangers of homogenization or any others, also of our time. Quite the opposite, it might be thought that there is something about these new ad hoc constructions of identities, made to measure and according to a particular situation, designed to promote and legitimize a particular response, but incapable — and this would be the serious part — of making sense of what happens and confronting the agents with their genuine responsibility (as agents). That is why at the moment when one has to measure oneself against the effective complexity of reality and put oneself in the place of someone who can do nothing other than take decisions, many of these discourses are obliged to call on the help of complementary terms or discourses, which apparently make them right in a way they are incapable of being on their own.

The same thing happens with the reiterated use of terms such as tolerance or the introduction of debates like the one on relativism, and that is the reason why I have given them a substantial amount of room in this book. Often the discourse of tolerance has played with that fallacy — that is, has uncritically accepted that ontologization of differences we mentioned a moment ago. By doing that, I was placing the argument in a territory that, rather than mistaken, is directly ambiguous, and incidentally passing on to the critics of tolerance the obligation to justify something they can in no way be called upon to do, while avoiding raising the basic questions that must inevitably be dealt with. Such would be the case when debating the possible paternalism contained in the word. There may be a paternalistic use of tolerance — who can doubt it? But it must be said that for such a use to occur we must first take for granted, if you will pardon the abrupt expression, an ontological exteriority, a situation in which we find ourselves in the face of entities that are essentially different from one another. Given that, the premise we are trying to introduce is that such a supposition implies an abuse, and that perhaps tolerance should use elements of another order and rank.

Kofi Annan, the former secretary general of the United Nations, began an article, published on the occasion of the 50th anniversary of the Universal Declaration of Human Rights ("Human rights, the fabric of our lives"), with the words that, about a century ago, were spoken by a slave from birth to a well-meaning anthropologist:

> I know your intentions are good. But I already have what you want to give me . . . You want to give me the right to be a man. I acquired that right when I was born. You, if you are stronger, can prevent me from living it, but you will never be able to give me something that belongs to me.

So anyone who defended tolerance toward a group of people, whomever they might be, would be acting like the anthropologist in the quotation. This disdainful, self-sufficient attitude is not appropriate, because there is no such hierarchy as this tolerant person supposes. There is no hierarchy; there is equality, specifically an equality in dignity — that dignity that authors like Manetti, Gelli, Pico della Mirandola or Luís Vives at the dawn of modernity had begun tentatively to theorize about. That is why true tolerance (or, which comes to the same thing, the tolerance we need today) is not paternalistic, nor does it imply that we disdainfully ignore others. With regard to those *others*, to other people, trying to use the link of tolerance probably creates more confusion than anything else. As has been said more than once, with a person one should not be tolerant but respectful. We should be tolerant of attitudes, behaviors or characteristics, of differences in short (which do not make the bearer, it is worth repeating, someone completely different, different as a whole). The appropriate attitude toward others is the one that best incorporates certain convictions. And if one of them is that we are radically equal, the right thing would be to adopt the attitude that best takes in that idea.

Equality is the right to difference — that is, the right to have a difference — not the right to be regarded as different, someone special, someone apart, from whom the same things cannot be required as from others, or from whom the same things we legitimately expect from everyone cannot be expected. On all too many occasions, a certain — it must be said, pseudoradical — rhetoric may have loaded such affirmations with negative connotations, when a correct reading would be exactly the opposite. Indeed, there is no more powerful, more radical idea than the idea of equality. There are few things we need more than to demand it. And, of course, there are few things we need less than alibis for inequality (like the kind concealed beneath the apparently analytical argument, much in circulation lately, according to which equality *will be given to us additionally* as an indirect and unwanted effect of the quest for freedom, that is if we scrupulously fulfill the requirement not to lift a finger in order to approach an egalitarian horizon).

But we will have to take the missing steps — which, indeed, lead once again to the question of identity. If other people matter to us it is because we perceive them as close to us, because we feel interested in them, because in the end we share elements of a common identity as people. Other people are never superfluous. We are equal with differences. That is why a condescending person is not truly tolerant, though on occasions he claims that classification for himself. To deserve it, he is lacking something essential: the conviction that the other he claims to tolerate is for him, in an important sense, one of his own. That is the element of truth contained in the ideas of all those authors (like Ariane Chebel d'Appollonia, or here in Spain, Manuel Delgado) who, perhaps with a slightly provocative formulation, demand the right to indifference.

Even though stating it may give rise to a misunderstanding, that demand must be unambiguously set in the sphere of the struggle against any form of exclusion. As are for those authors, for example, many of the apparent apologies for difference that end up helping to spread racist attitudes and behaviors in society, albeit a less aggressive racism than the old kind, an amiable, folkloric racism with a human face or low-intensity racism (however you prefer to call it), but racism nonetheless. Faced with that, the demand alludes to the right not to be the object of special treatment, to be regarded to all intents and purposes as a citizen like other citizens; that is, the owner of rights on terms of equality with anyone else.

Does that mean giving less importance to differences or confusing equality with identity? That is not the aim, of course: that is another debate on which we already have an abundant literature — we need only think of the gender studies that have so proliferated in recent years. The aim is, rather, to warn about some of the new clothes certain old discourses tend to dress in these days; above all, to draw attention to the fact, new in a sense, that all too frequently the attribution of the status of *different* is an alibi for exclusion (if not for self-exclusion). And so, to give just one example, in practice a notion like ethnic minority usually fulfills the function of organizing social marginality and cheap labor legally and politically. The warning consists of realizing to what extent one of the factors that most powerfully contributes to legitimizing inequality is precisely a mistaken conception — in terms of size and nature — of identity.

In the end, in the apparently formal, almost conventional, affirmation that the construction of identity is a process, we find the antidote for those excesses. For if we acknowledge our complex, heterogeneous, historical condition we shall find it difficult to put forward ideas that distinguish, tacitly or implicitly, between first- and second-class identities. It will be argued that hardly anyone dares do that nowadays, but it would be worth analyzing to what extent certain ways of dealing with the problem of cultural clashes often seem to operate with the image that the clash is like a battle between two armies, each of which is made up of a contingent of individuals equipped with an unambiguous and homogeneous identity. We should say explicitly that nobody is of a piece, and that, applied to the problem we are concerned with now, becomes an affirmation that we must think of identity as the setting for the conflict rather than a well-defined protagonist of it.

To talk like this is inevitably to summarize. In matters of this kind the right — and the prudent — way is to formulate things in terms of tendencies, among other reasons because those conflicts occur in an extraordinary variety of situations. But it would not be good for a fear of simplifying to condemn us to endless nuances or, worse still, an inane deliberation that would prevent any minimally categorical statement. It might be better to tend toward a kind of formulation that deals with the real shapes in which the processes we have mentioned occur today. And, as we were saying a moment ago, just as today we are all multicultural (which in no way means there is no longer a problem, or that it has lost intensity, just that it is tending to shift in another direction: toward us, ourselves), it would also be worth reconsidering whether it is a good idea to keep using terms like "ethnocentrism" or "Eurocentrism," insofar as they may be anachronically spatial, geographical. Perhaps the sole justification for keeping them in circulation is their residual usefulness as a reminder of the origin, provided that is not confused with a real location in some part of the planet or another.

Just as some time ago North and South ceased to be cardinal points of the compass and became concepts loaded with valuations, so the unstoppable processes of globalization of the different spheres of human activity make it advisable to tone down terms like the ones mentioned, or at least keep them for situations in which the conflicts are still closely linked to the territory, for example because there is a dispute over the ownership of the land, as in some countries in Latin America today. Apart from such cases — and given that the occupation of the planet was taken as concluded some time ago — the efficacy of maintaining those old labels is doubtful. To become entangled in trying to spot the Eurocentricity of the discourse — not to mention the way of life — of an African-American who has been settled in the United States for generations, of a German citizen of Turkish origin, or any other similar case, does not seem to be the most fruitful approach to the issue.

What would be fruitful, however, is an approach that takes into account the present realities and, from them, is capable of suitably describing the different forms of conflict. To do so it is no longer any use settling for a generic affirmation — almost a declaration of principle — that in a sense we are all mongrels. Nor is it enough to maintain that cultures themselves are mongrel. Those are valid starting points, but not enough unless they go on to explain how, despite that shared mongrel condition, situations we regard as totally unacceptable continue to arise.

There are no simple answers to that concern, because the problems that give rise to it are not simple. Theses unanimously accepted today in all kinds of intellectual circles such as the growing complexity of reality are binding and generate long-term theoretical effects. It would certainly be mistaken to place all these emerging problems at the service of a new homogenization (culturalist, as we might call it) or, worse still, a new ontological reductionism of the social. The emergence of new conflicts and the appearance of new players with a will to transform themselves into subjects (i.e. the protagonists of their own destiny) should in no event serve to liquidate old problems or decree the disappearance of old players. It could serve to correct some of the most serious mistakes we have inherited or to detect possible new situations.

The dangers of exclusion should not be insisted on at the cost of forgetting or downgrading other realities such as exploitation, domination or oppression. All of them should be thought of as processes — of a heterogeneous nature: economic, political, sexual or any other — that may occur simultaneously and the complex structures of which need to be analyzed in the light of the sweeping transformations that have taken place in the world recently. But however that may be, what we can say now is that any attempt to turn some of the new social players separately, or the new social movements as a whole, into the *new revolutionary subject*, who could step in to replace the ones that have been defeated in this last stretch of history, would be an endeavor as useless as it is mistaken.

Probably none of them still clings to the expectation of universality, so typical of some of the old subjects (above all, those who thought of themselves as the supreme revolutionary subject), but that should not hasten us to a defeatist conclusion. That none of them wants to take on the task of leading the whole of humanity to a better destiny single-handed does not mean that they are not interested in the global transformation of the existing state of affairs.

The new subjects, and their new identities, are only weaker than those of the past in appearance. In fact, the affirmation we have already emphasized, that nobody is of a piece, not only is more descriptive of the genuine reality of today's subjects but also allows them to assume the complexity of reality on better terms. One is not just a woman, or indigenous, or a worker, or a young person, or any other trait, but all of those things at the same time, in a specific, changing structure, generating one's own effects and being a differentiated object of the actions of others. For the same reason, affirmations of the "first and foremost I am … (here whatever characteristic it may be) … and after that" kind are probably not the right ones either: they smack of essentialism, as if, aside from history, some aspect of one's own identity that is more transcendental than another could be predetermined. It might be more in keeping with what we have been saying to maintain that the different aspects are *foregrounded*, demanding their share of the limelight. The recent past has provided us with enough samples of the errors a rigidly unambiguous concept of subjectivity can lead to, errors from which we should draw the appropriate lesson: economic transformations of a progressive nature that have left patriarchal structures intact, apparently indigenist ideas that take no account of class conflicts, feminist demands that are put forward as prepolitical, and so forth.

On the other hand, it would be equally inappropriate to be content to say that the world as such has burst into a thousand pieces, that the language of totalities has expired irreversibly because we are definitively installed in the age of the fragment. Perhaps what that language, with its deeply defeatist connotations, is really telling us is the difficulty we have facing up to the new complexities, those orders of meaning that in a way were unthinkable until now. But the impossibility, and far less the meaninglessness, of any kind of action — including that variety of collective action that is political action — by no means follow from that. What does follow, of course, is the need to think about it in terms of the new subjects, the new realities and the new objectives.

If today, to give just one example (but a particularly stark one), we tend to speak both of social exclusion and of the new danger stalking us, it is partly because in many countries the combination of technological development, with the inevitable aftermath of the mass destruction of jobs, and certain neoliberal policies are driving large sectors of the population into marginal territories. There is something new about this phenomenon in more than one sense. First, the determination to commodify all social relations is showing no respect for spheres that, in the traditional liberal discourse of authors like John Stuart Mill, should have been kept safe from the market precisely as a guarantee that it would operate more efficiently. Second, the disproportionate scope of social exclusion goes far beyond the bounds of what Marx called the "lumpenproletariat," whose function as a market regulator restricted its importance in a certain way. Here we are looking at a phenomenon of such magnitude that some authors (specifically Viviane Forrester) have coined the concept *economic horror* to refer to the sufferings of the part of the world population living in conditions of marginality. One idea beginning to gain ground is that there is something worse than the exploitation of man by man: the lack of exploitation, the cruel fact that a whole set of human beings are regarded as superfluous (for lack of jobs). Thus grows a new fear: to go from exploitation to exclusion.

This situation has repercussions on different sectors of society in a way that is not always identical to how it would have been in similar circumstances in the past, and those different repercussions are what must be urgently confronted. In some countries in Latin America, for instance, the processes of commodification (which in that part of the world is called privatization) is hitting the indigenous population especially hard, pushing them to the very verge of extinction. In others the entrenchment of wars is forcing women to take on (once again) all the burdens of the family, from household tasks to the economy, by way of the education of the children and others, thus giving rise to processes that some people have called the *feminization of poverty*, and so forth.

It is not a matter of shifting the register of this introduction toward specific political or socioeconomic issues: that would run the risk of the (highly likely) inadequacy of the descriptions and the odd wrong analysis unnecessarily damaging hypotheses that hold up without that assistance. What we are trying to do is draw attention to the scope and nature of a tendency and the consequent need to modify certain categories and approaches. And so, to recover the thread we are interested in, the affirmation of the mobile, plastic, open character of identity must not be understood as an ultimate conclusion beyond which no more can be said; rather the opposite, it should mark a new starting point from which to begin to pose the pressing questions of the day in another way.

The thesis that identity — any identity, of course — is a construction should in no event lead us to a pessimistic conclusion: quite the reverse. Affirming our condition as products — even artifacts, to use a more radical expression — does not necessarily lead to any disdainfully pejorative consideration of subjects and their identities, but to a register of quite another kind. For the content of the affirmation also implies that in our hands, with all the mediations and nuances you like, lies the power to determine the autonomous or heteronomous character of the construction. Knowing that our identity is a product is really a question that forces us to decide whether or not we want to take part in that production, and how.

Those very programmatic ideas the Renaissance thinkers had about human dignity may well conserve the validity of the accurate intuition — the flash that, for a moment, allows us to perceive contours and outlines clearly — but must be applied to our present conditions to tell us the precise element of truth they still contain. If you like, we can continue to accept with the authors mentioned earlier that the dignity of man lies in his freedom, understood as the power to shape his own being, provided we do not make that idea an essentialist interpretation, as if everyone had the seed of a preexisting *self*, which could become reality simply by proposing it.

For us, today, the observation that the power to shape one's own being requires objective material conditions has become a commonplace; otherwise everything that has gone before becomes mere *flatus vocis* or, still worse, a consoling, deceitful ideology. In other words, the idea of human dignity is useful, has collective efficacy, if it contributes to the emergence of policies of equality. But if equality in dignity means equality in the *right to be*, besides contributing to an attempt to make the old dream of men designing their own ends according to their preferences come true, such policies should also safeguard the exercise of that right. For freedom, by its very nature, gives rise to differences.

Here there is a tension — a Kantian tension, in the end — from which we must not abdicate, which makes the link with responsibility necessary, inescapable. For responsibility is, indeed, taking charge. Taking charge of everything that has to do with one, beginning with oneself, with that particular fabric of projects, wishes, interests and desires we call identity. Society, obviously, must offer the conditions for each person to develop his inalienable capacity to choose his own ends and determine his own life plan, among other reasons because such tasks are only possible in a particular society and culture. That, as Luís Villoro has suggested, could be called the right to belong, and there should be no reservations about it if it is understood as the right to non-exclusion.

But it should be emphasized that it is a right, and not an obligation, particularly in view of some forms of understanding collective identity that have been proliferating lately and seem to be proposing a quality of links between individuals and the group so severe that we might even think they are links that *have to be fulfilled* by the individual. Not to feel as if one belongs to the group, the fatherland, the nation or the culture in all forms and in the way the relevant powers decide has in many places become the antechamber of another form of exclusion. The right to belong is part of a right, greater if you will, to one's own identity. And if we have just said that that identity is constructed, we must add next that everyone constructs it by exercising their freedom, which also means deciding what their different spheres of belonging are.

Cohesion cannot be the new label for reintroducing a now indefensible social uniformity. The constellation of the different spheres that make up human life (work, affections, religious beliefs, politics . . .) exploded long ago and there is no way back from that explosion. We could allude to Baudelaire, Benjamin or so many episodes of this late modernity to show the irreversible character of the process or the different ways in which individuals in our big cities have assumed in their own being the fragmentation of the old unity of life and the complete exteriority the fragments have been left in. If the point is to defend cohesion — because we agree that we must oppose any form of exclusion — we must say that there is no better way of conceiving social cohesion than accepting what Havel has called the individual's different spheres of belonging (from the most private to the most cosmopolitan, by way of the city, the country or the nation-state). And those spheres do not need a preliminary sketch or preestablished form of harmony (as the WASP — white Anglo-Saxon Protestant — model in US society might have been at one time or, on a more general level, the white-male-adult triad as the definition of "man"). We can return to our previous affirmation that no one is of a piece and add that perhaps the best of all possible worlds would be the one in which we had in our hands the possibility of arranging the many pieces we are composed of in the order we decided (or felt we were in a condition to bear).

Things have been dispatched to an uncertain future, because the difficulty of such an expectation is plain to see. But humanity has lived with punishment for a long time — its whole history, to be exact — and the problems of today should not come as new. Difficulty has never been a conclusive argument against action and, therefore, from the difficulties that may arise from this particular expectation we should extract arguments for persevering with the task. The ones provided so far have tended to highlight the importance of and the need for it. It may be that an introduction need go no further. It may be up to the book as such to take the next step and persuade the reader that the task of taking charge of his own world (with him in it) is, as well as important and necessary, the most desirable one.

CHAPTER 1

The Problem that Concerns Us: Responsibility and Identity

For some time we have known that philosophy is lagging behind the world. But we sometimes forget that philosophy can also lag behind itself. That is what happens when certain issues like *the return of the subject* or *the need for a fresh look at individualism* — which seem to suggest a pendular, if not a directly random, conception of the history of ideas — are raised as items *on the agenda*. If we are to stay with those labels, the first thing to be aware of is their extreme antiquity. We need only remember Riesman, Sennett or the Popperian debate on methodological individualism. It therefore seems that we must modify the approach. The (twofold) question we should face is, first, what is new in thought so that we can be sure we are not dealing with the same thing and, second, to what extent the reality our schemas are supposed to apply themselves to is also the same. But while we could answer the first one by saying that the axis of the debate may have shifted from the methodological individualism / methodological holism antagonism to the methodological monism / methodological pluralism opposition (the latter represented by those who defend fusions of paradigm and the like), in the case of the second we would have to begin by acknowledging that it is fundamentally the changes in the plane of reality that authorize us to think about certain issues in a different way. The concepts of progress and backwardness seem to have lost much of their usefulness. There is no precise criterion for discerning when the philosopher is acting as a mere apologist or ideologist and when he is being a forerunner. The shadow of Hegel's owl stretches too long at dawn. Perhaps we can only say that philosophical discourse, which had analyzed the theoretical conditions of possibility of some categories and discourses, has found that their material conditions of possibility have occurred,[1] and that in the confrontation between them there has not always been agreement. But while that disagreement may be valued as a sign of the obsolescence or the error of the categories, in the opposite case it would be best to say that the intuitions or anticipations in question *have reached their truth*. This idea would serve to introduce the meaning of the new direction discourse should take. The point, of course, is not to fall back into the typical ideas of the last decade of the kind propounded by Ferry, Renaut and so many others that they could all be included under the heading *crisis of the subject and postmodernity*. At least we should speak now of two new factors that oblige us to look at this issue of the individual/subjectivity in new terms: first, the apparently definitive failure of a model of society, with its enormous economic, social, political and ideological repercussions, and, second, the crisis of the welfare state that has been occurring in developed European countries. Evidently both factors are deeply connected, but we are going to tug the end of the second one to try to unravel the theoretical ball of wool we have proposed.

A second observation, derived directly from the previous one: in the matters we are going to refer to, the distinction between micro and macro levels may not be very useful. The new problems people are facing today transcend both political frontiers and theoretical demarcation lines. AIDS, drug addiction, world famine or the destruction of the ozone layer are global, planetary situations, to a large extent new ones — "challenges" they are called in a somewhat more emphatic language — that seem to generate a kind of specific perplexity. The inertia of so many years invited us to think (or, rather, to believe without thinking) that some authority, institution or public organism should take charge of them because — the argument ran — it is in the nature of (social) things that each problem has an appointed negotiator for its solution. But these situations have demolished the schema. First, because their magnitude goes far beyond the real possibilities of any state (however much it may be disposed to be a benefactor); second, because in the face of them the inevitable question arises: is anyone responsible for them?

And so, since we are asking, is what is happening here very different in the case of individual problems? In this other case, starting from an apparently different (and sometimes opposite) situation we come to a similar conclusion, to wit, in this sphere too individuals are less and less faced with their responsibility. The administration and public services frequently take on their obligations through documents, time limits, requests, forwarding. The legal institutions split, the law becomes bureaucratic and in ten years nobody remembers what actually happened, the reason why someone was sanctioned. We could say that infringements become virtual. Just think of what happened in France in the 1990s with the case of the contaminated blood, or in Spain in the 1980s with the massive poisoning caused by the sale of industrial-grade rapeseed oil for human consumption. It is not a matter of talking about punishment.[2] Something similar has happened with political corruption and financial speculation: the newspapers regularly tell us about the speculative practices of people who buy companies and obtain profits from the capital without having any money (or at least without risking their own). Property, financial or spiritual, has to a large extent become a fraud. It is no longer necessary to invest in order to produce. Or, returning to the general, it is no longer necessary to commit oneself physically or affectively in order to think or decide personally about any event. So that seems to be the sign of the times: it is increasingly difficult, on whatever the level, to impute anything to anybody, but at the same time there is usually agreement (which is a good thing) that the evils caused should be put right.

These statements are no more than an initial layout, a quick sketch, about which some questions should be raised. Such as, what does the concept of responsibility commit one to? What are its theoretical costs? Is it, as we believe, a central concept for an understanding of our reality or, on the contrary, as other people think,[3] should its persistence be interpreted as a mere remnant of the old discourses, a categorical imaginary that refuses to disappear? There is, why hide it, a merely theoretical, generalist approach to this question, which eludes subjectifying the material conditions of existence of subjects and the ways they have changed in recent times. This is the gnoseological approach, which focuses on an examination of the exclusively discursive nature of the category, its similarities to and differences from other apparently close ones, and so forth. This approach is not lacking in interest, which means we shall have to say something about it later, albeit in passing. Among other reasons, it may provide us with elements to answer the first two questions. But answering the third, let us anticipate this now, will force us to complete the perspective with other approaches in which *what is happening* has been examined from a point of view I am not sure whether to call sociological, ethical or directly historical . . .

The best thing would be to begin with a strong statement: none of the foregoing considerations are really useful without an open affirmation of the central place — with regard to the meaning of the action — occupied by the identity of the agent. This is not an attempt to dismiss a highly complex issue with a programmatic stroke of the pen, since it involves arguments that are far from being settled (such as the theoretical validity of determinism or how the requirement of being a person, which some demand to allocate the authorship of an action, is met). But it does pinpoint the roads we know lead nowhere. For example, does the supposedly modern (very 1970s, to be exact) idea according to which the subject and his corresponding identity are no more than a construction, the result of a series of processes of social interaction, have anything to add to the debate? What else could they be once we have renounced nativism or any other variant of Cartesian essentialism?

A trivial example may allow us to intuitively catch the meaning of this. For there to be a film image, 18 frames per second are required, as I understand it. There is a necessary, but in no way sufficient, condition here. For once we have established the materiality of the image, we have to say that behind that number there is only celluloid, a mere physical support. The discourse, the story, the poetics or even the semiotics of film appear as soon as that natural requirement has been fulfilled. Likewise, it could be said, the question is not — we should even ask ourselves was it ever? — the materials the subject is made of, but the nature of the product once constituted, its features, its possible autonomy, the real importance of its intervention in the medium, and so forth. Or, better still, the proof a contrario: what degree of intelligibility (or unintelligibility) do human behaviors reach when we give up thinking in terms of subjectivity?

One particular form of that renunciation is the one we find widespread in many supposedly social discourses these days. Enzensberger has criticized it harshly in his latest book. In his opinion, developed European countries are witnessing a curious historical phenomenon: "in the twilight of social democracy, Rousseau has triumphed again." It is not the means of production that have been nationalized, but therapy. In *Civil War* Enzensberger proposes to confront the rhetoric that systematically exculpates the criminal by passing on the responsibility to his home or the absence of one, to his father's strictness or his weakness, to an excess or lack of love, to the authoritarianism or antiauthoritarianism of his teachers, or to the consumer society or bad audiovisual examples, and the full panoply of lazy, contradictory justifications to exonerate the person from any commitment to his own life. The degree of exculpation has become so mechanical and grotesque that Enzensberger wonders ironically whether criminals from the extermination camps such as Höss or Mengele would now be defenseless victims "in need of sympathy and perhaps psychotherapeutic treatment paid for by the social security." The quotation ends thus: "Following that logic, only therapists could raise moral doubts about it, since they are the only ones capable of understanding the situation. And since everyone else is not responsible for anything, far less for their own acts, they no longer exist as people, just as beneficiaries of social security."[4] Here is a particular new example of Ortega's "barbarism of specialization" that we have reached, not through the development of technology, but paradoxically through a largely speculative process of gutting the idea of identity.

But it must be said, to avoid any misunderstandings, that the way of renouncing subjectivity (and therefore removing responsibility) pointed out by Enzensberger is just one of the many that are characteristic of our time. To insist too much on that could lead to confusing valuations, such as interpreting that the serious aspect of this process is the extent to which it is the end of a period when justice was still a desirable horizon, when attempts were made to have good prevail over evil and it was believed that the crime would receive its punishment in the end. But all this, as we know all too well, was only a white lie (when it was not an organized deceit) for which we should feel no nostalgia whatever. It is therefore not appropriate to reproach this argument with being conservative. What we are talking about now is a process of a general order, which almost constitutes the social.

In fact, we would have to argue that the abandonment of subjectivity is one of the most typical characteristics of the world today, and especially of the way in which people live their participation in it. It is true that our modern permissive societies say that they are striving to achieve the free development of the individual, but what we should ask is why, despite the emphasis in the statement, they do not seem to be even approaching that goal. The answer we propose is implicit in all we have said so far. There is no possibility of access to the goals this society proclaims from the subjective conditions the same society promotes. The individuals of the permissive era see how from the mass media — and especially through advertising — all the preconceived models of person are being destroyed. The market needs consumers with maximum plasticity, ready to bow to the changing plans of an advertising system that unbalances and multiplies desire, makes it unstable and fleeting.[5] Weak subjects, in short, incapable of setting targets for which they would need a strong identity.

A true indicator of their weakness is the banality of the gestures asked of them to cooperate on the solution of problems of undoubted seriousness. The red ribbon is the extent of their solidarity with AIDS sufferers, the badge on the lapel with the relevant slogan constitutes their contribution to the struggle against racism and attendance at the concert given by their favorite rock group (whom they would have gone to see in any case) proclaims to all and sundry their support for a good cause. They are all light rituals that remove responsibility: ways of everyday self-exculpation that do not require the slightest sacrifice. We do not intend to hint at, or much less reintroduce, an opposition between hedonism and self-denial (which would have unmistakably Christian resonances), simply to put on record the way in which a certain discourse tries to resolve or evade crucial difficulties, the way in which, specifically, it tackles those major problems for any ethics that are natural evil and (possibly) social evil. It is obvious that the individual's right to his own happiness could not be postulated without restrictions.

But what needs emphasizing now is that there is nothing more operative, more functional in this context, than an individual who gives up any expectation of shaping his own identity. We should even add that there is nothing easier: a host of discourses would come to his aid. Let us also think of the postmodernists of different feathers, the authors with an analytical training (the controversial Derek Parfit[6] would be the outstanding exponent) who reject the idea of the permanent, continuous, stable *I* and propose in its place a multiple, discontinuous, heterogeneous *I* who is under no obligation to recognize himself in that agent of the past to whom third parties attribute a particular behavior. There is no reason to reconstruct a whole controversy that is certainly complex. To our way of thinking, the fundamental question is this: is this testimony of this individual, estranged from his past *I*, irrefutable proof that we really have no right to speak of the same person? Irrefutable, of course not. Because, for whatever reason, that plurality of *Is* should be defensible in any contexts. And it is curious that what seems to function (better or worse) for the past does not do so at all for the future. When, for instance, our expectations are threatened, few of us find relief in the thought that "the future *I* will be another one." Or even more, that plurality of *Is* is not defended alike in all past situations. So, for example, just as it is easy to hear arguments of this kind to lift the burden of an uncomfortable past ("I'm no longer the same person as then . . .", "I don't understand how I was capable of doing such a thing . . ."), it is absolutely unusual to find them when goodness or merit are attributed. In those cases the same old subjectivist rhetoric reappears on those very lips, even quite shamelessly ("I always intended to . . .", "I would like to thank those who have always trusted in me . . ."). All of which leads us to think that in fact the function of those antisubjectivist arguments is to provide ad hoc alibis with which to escape a hypothetical attribution of responsibility. And so it is the effects and consequences of that escape that Enzensberger has tried to show through his waspish analyses. And that is also the perspective from which we must interpret his demand for a return to full personal responsibility. Now, to be in tune with the new times, that responsibility cannot be confined to a mere revamping of the old theories of responsibility — for example, more Weber. Indeed, in a rather special sense the discourse about responsibility is something strictly new. Until now when people spoke of it they did so in the light of suppositions that are no longer the case. For example, they started from the idea that the scope of human action, and therefore human responsibility, was strictly limited. But, as Hannah Arendt repeats in different passages from her work, the action is, by its very nature, "unlimited" in its consequences and "unpredictable" in its ultimate results, because man "acts in an environment where every reaction is a chain reaction."[7] And hardly anything changes when will is introduced into the schema. Not only are we overwhelmed by the consequences of our heedless acts but also it is in the essence of action to produce unforeseeable and incalculable effects. In other words, also Arendt's: "human action produces consequences ad infinitum." We are not looking at a mere anticipation of the thesis, so fashionable lately, of perverse or unwanted effects. Nor one of those affirmations, so much to the taste of philosophers, that confine themselves to noting the complexity of everything (anything that is being talked about). The matter goes deeper.

Today things have changed irreversibly as far as the Weberian approach is concerned. Modern technology has propitiated actions of a previously unthinkable magnitude, has introduced new objects and brought about new consequences, so that it could well be said that the panorama of the whole world has been transformed. As Hans Jonas has pointed out, so far "the good and evil about which action had to care lay close to the act, either in the praxis or in its immediate reach, and were not matters for remote planning."[8] And so it was thought idle speculation to stop to think about the remote consequences our actions might have in some unknown destiny. Ethics preferred to concentrate on the moral quality of the momentary act itself, in which we had to take account of the right of the neighbor who lived beside us. But,

> the nature of human action has *de facto* changed, and that an object of an entirely new order — no less than the whole biosphere of the planet — has been added to what we must be responsible for because of our power over it. And of what surpassing importance an object, dwarfing all previous objects of active man! Nature as a human responsibility is surely a *novum* to be pondered in ethical theory.[9]

It is therefore not a matter of a change in scale for the same thing, but a deepening, to the ultimate consequences we are capable of perceiving, of two determinations often sidelined in the old ideas: first, the fact that we must demand responsibility for what is not done and, second, the importance of those to whom we must answer for our actions. But both determinations, it should be emphasized, can irrupt into the discourse in their own right precisely because, so to speak, those changes in the landscape of the world have proved the truth of Arendt's assertions. That new object over which, thanks to technology, we have power in our hands with no change to the characteristic features of human action — that is, its "extraordinary fragility and lack of reliability." Indeed, if to that we add that "although we do not know what we are doing, we have no possibility of undoing what we have done,"[10] that is the irreversible nature of the action, the outcome that would seem to be looming is that of a humanity irremediably doomed to ruin and destruction.

Arendt, however, does not surrender to fate and it is the way she defends herself from it that takes us to the core of her argument. Her hope seems to be related to ontology: the most typical feature of the human condition is a capacity to start something in the world.[11] Men are beings that set goals, propose ends. It is that very power of initiative that is designated through the term natality. Natality expresses the ontological foundation of each human individual. Every person is unique because, as Arendt argues in *The Human Condition*, "with each birth something singularly new comes into the world."[12] But that affirmation does not end up in any form of solipsism, any pigeonholing of the individual in a supposed foundational difference. "With word and deed we insert ourselves into the human world, and this insertion is like a second birth, in which we confirm and take upon ourselves the naked fact of our original physical appearance." The new beginning inherent to birth makes itself felt in the world because the newcomer exercises his capacity to start something new — in other words, to act. If one prefers the other way around: "a life without speech and without action [. . .] is literally dead to the world; it has ceased to be a human life because it is no longer lived among men."[13]

On the clear understanding that the word we are alluding to is precisely *the word of action*. For Arendt silent action does not exist (or if it exists it is irrelevant). Without words, action loses the actor, and by losing him it loses itself insofar as it is action. The ultimate content of her thesis that "action is intensely personal" is this: action without a *who* linked to it is lacking in meaning. The link may be unequally aware — this is not the place to go into this, simply to note it — but, in one way or another, it has to be. For the world only becomes fully human through the initiatives of agents. And the agent of the acts is only possible, she claims, insofar as he is also the person who speaks the words, who is identified as the actor and announces what he is doing, what he has done and what he is trying to do. This is the general setting for everything we dealt with earlier. Though we need to go further. These Arendtian affirmations can be easily interpreted as the ontological-anthropological foundation absent in Jonas's ethical idea. Just as his contributions to the imperative of responsibility can be valued as the most plausible ethical development from Arendt's premises. In any event, for our purposes it will be enough to persevere in the case in which the coincidence of the two ideas seems clearest: the idea of action is inseparable from the idea of responsibility.

But such a responsibility — how could it be otherwise? — must depend on the action that, bearing in mind what we have said, also means depending on its protagonists. That is how we can recover the full meaning of the precise question we were discussing: we are responsible not so much for what we have done but for what we do not do to prevent the growing deterioration of the human habitat. And we are responsible to future generations for the natural, political and cultural inheritance we bequeath them. One can observe the growing difference between earlier arguments and ethics of responsibility, which confined themselves to pointing out that one is responsible for one's acts and their immediate consequences (but not for what is beyond what one can and must do), without assuming the determinations we are talking about. Faced with them, the ethic we may infer from all this would be an ethic "directed at the future," provided that is not understood in the sense that we have to conceive an ethic to be practiced by men in the future (if we allow there to be any). Rather the opposite, this hypothetical ethic should be governed precisely by the men of today; it would be, as Jonas says in another of his books, "a present day ethic that takes care of the future, that sets out to protect our descendants from the consequences of our present actions."

This direction can be inferred, it will hardly be necessary to stress, not as a result of the surprising irruption into the discourse of values such as solidarity, but as a strict consequence of the efficacy of the suppositions submitted. It is the practical way of trying to find an outlet for the explosive coexistence of power and fragility, efficacy and weakness, knowledge and irreversibility, so characteristic of the world today. There is therefore no appeal to transcendent or exterior entities. The responsibility we must confront does not spring from the demands of any ideal of perfection. On the contrary, it flowers from pure love of the world[14] (an Augustinian nexus shared by Arendt and Jonas) and a passion for knowledge. See, by way of example, the two preliminary duties of this future-oriented ethic; the first is to visualize the effects in the long run; the second, to "educate our soul to a willingness to let itself be affected by the mere thought of possible fortunes and calamities of future generations."[15] This proposal could, in the old style, deserve the classification of materialist, if it were not because it seems to be moved by an ethical variant of the most metaphysical of questions, "why something and not nothing?" — only transformed here into a demand: we have an obligation to try to see that there is something and not nothing. But let us alight once more on the debate; let us retrieve the terms of the imaginary controversy. Someone might think that a convincing way of dodging all those duties might be to allege that he himself, in turn, received an already degraded legacy and, therefore, he is not morally obliged to concern himself about those who are to come.[16] One would be mistaken to trust the argument: the allegation is decidedly Peter Pannish. To exculpate oneself is to refuse to grow, to cling to a place that now belongs to others.[17] The words, once again, may give rise to confusion. Are we supposed to understand that the responsibility of the world to young people means adults accepting it as it is? Is such a thing tantamount to denying adults the possibility of wishing, openly or secretly, for a different world? If that were so, it would seem that what is being proposed is an absolute decline of our right to alter the course of events. But that is not so. In fact it is radically the opposite. If we turn the terms on their heads the idea emerges more clearly: where does the conviction that nothing contributes more effectively to changing the world than shaping young people's minds in a revolutionary way come from? By now we have seen too many models of the *construction of the new man* fail to keep trusting ingenuously in that expectation. Arendt would no doubt react with irritation today to this supposedly nice image, so often repeated in the media, of the father on the demonstration with a small child hoisted on his shoulders, bearing the banner, slogan or poster his progenitor has decided he has to hold up before even having the slightest awareness of where he is.[18] Here, our author might say, we have a perverse way of staying with the old.

In the face of this attitude, she calls on adults to assume responsibility for the world in which they have placed the next generation, and she does so for a reason. If in the eyes of young people adults in general and educators in particular seem like representatives of the world it is precisely because they have been introduced by adults into a world in constant change. There is no room for another distribution of roles. The temptation of juvenility, so strong for one generation, is a lost battle against time and against history. It is, in a sense that has to be qualified, a strictly reactionary temptation. For if our hope always lies in the element of novelty provided by each generation, and only in that, there is nothing more terrible than to destroy it by channeling it in the direction we adults want it to go in. And, the other side of the coin, nothing more typical of the human condition (since "it is in the nature of the human condition that the world is created by mortals to be their dwelling for a limited time") than being careful and gentle with this seed of novelty of which each child is the bearer.

It is not — the quotation in brackets leaves little room for confusion — a matter of starting from scratch every time, of each generation wiping clean the slate of the past, or anything of that kind. It is more a matter of pointing our historical action in the right direction for each generation to develop the possibility it brings with it. That is why education is one of the best examples of the difficulties that action runs into: in the educational process adults assume responsibility for the child's life and development, but also, inseparably, for the continuity of reality. At that moment, in short, when men have to test their love for the world, when they have to show whether they want to save it from the ruin the absence of other people would mean. It is a rather thorny position, as opposed to how it might seem at first glance. In fact, it decidedly confronts certain commonplaces that are deeply entrenched in many supposedly progressive ways of thinking. "Be realistic, demand the impossible"? Arendt no doubt had a reply. It appears for the first time in *The Origins of Totalitarianism* and we can find it repeated in *History and Immortality*: "everything is possible" is the idea that most deeply defines Nazi discourse. With its opposite, the fantasy of perfection, the utopian dream, it is a variation of death. That emphasized property of human action consisting of introducing something new, something that had never been before, something unexpected, surprising — that is, unpredictable, into the world time and again has an absolutely unavoidable corollary: the frustration of expectations.

In a way it could be said that we have not made much progress: we are looking at the ultimate theoretical effects of the premise of natality. They all follow from the fact of the constant appearance of individuals who *are beginning*, who with their indeterminable opening close the way to the utopian illusion. Unless, as Jonas remarks with a certain degree of sarcasm,[19] the utopia achieved proceeds to abolish birth. Arendt thinks the same way, but expresses it more categorically (almost brutally): utopia, she writes in *The Human Condition*, is the real opium of the people.[20] To interpret that attitude solely in political terms of possibilism or moderation (social-democratic or any other) would be to miss the point. She is thinking of action within history and denounces — in a way some critics have called determinedly antimodern[21] — the ideology of progress to annihilate freedom. That is the deep meaning of her famous affirmation (in "Understanding and Politics," precisely) that "history is a tale that never ceases to begin but never ends." Neither invincible fate nor devastating contingency. The generations that follow us are the only surface on which we can write the future. The new man, if such an expectation still makes any sense, is neither constructed nor produced: he is allowed to be.

But it is exactly when making statements of this order that we need to remember that at no time have we spoken of guilt, only of responsibility[22] — and responsibility is not arbitrary. It has been said: with technology, actions — even if no longer exclusively those of the individual subject — have an unprecedented causal scope that affects the future. To which we have to add capacities for prediction, incomplete as always, but that go beyond any previous ones. For its part, irreversibility has been heightened by what Jonas has called "the indefinitely cumulative propagation of the effects of technological practice."[23] There is, in the end, the evident magnitude of remote effects. All those transformations in reality force us to reconsider the content of the old categories. Autonomy, today, means far more than the mere capacity to fend for ourselves: it means showing that we have a certain power. That is precisely what makes us responsible in our own right. The least of it now is whether or not this reality is the result of our actions. What matters is that it is in our hands to prevent a certain future, provide the means for preventing the deterioration from becoming a disaster. The question "who was it?" we now see was only valid for immediate phenomena. But for the serious threats that loom over our environment, the question that needs an urgent answer is another: "how to avoid it?"

It is time to go back to the beginning. We started our reconstruction of the debate by alluding to a way of posing these subjects that was so characteristic of the previous decade. It could even be argued that it was one of its teachings: after so many critical reviews the category of subject is indispensable to reach some form of intelligibility of what is happening to us, especially the part of what is happening to us we call history.[24] But it is up to us to expand the teachings we have received. I would go so far as to argue that today it is not only knowledge but also, and most of all, the *very possibility of human action* in the world that is committed in that specific defense of the subject that is indissolubly linked to the concept of responsibility. That may well be the most truthful summary of what I have tried to say.

I remember having heard the late Manuel Sacristán, commenting on the need to review conventional political categories some years ago, say that the term "conservative" had become a deeply inappropriate one: the only thing the conservatives of our day conserve is the property register, he pointed out ironically. It was a way of saying that the compulsion to transform had ceased to be progressive, of warning that we were entering a period when the only horizon remaining for those who once fought for emancipation may well be the mere defense of the survival of the human race. Linking this to the issues I have tried to develop, a rephrasing — I would like to think a respectful one — of the old thesis occurred to me: so far men have devoted themselves to changing the world, the point now is to take charge of it.

Notes

1. A convincing argument for what we are simply mentioning here is provided by the much trumpeted Anthony Giddens in his book *The Consequences of Modernity* (Cambridge: Cambridge University Press, 1990), when he analyzes the new social circumstances people have to cope with today. His conclusion is that we live in a *radicalized modernity* rather than postmodernity (which in no way means that he says that a postmodern order is unthinkable) and that consequently, far from being driven into a corner, categories like subjectivity must be seen in this new light (the discovery of oneself becomes a project directly related to the reflectiveness of modernity).

2. Referring to Nazi Germany, Hannah Arendt had pointed out the distances that separate this notion from the notion of responsibility in her work "Organized Guilt and Universal Responsibility," recently republished in the volume *Hannah Arendt: Essays in Understanding 1930–1954* (New York: Harcourt Brace & Co, 1994), pp. 121–32. The first version was published as an article under the title "German Guilt" (*Jewish Frontier*, no. 12, 1945).

3. For example, to mention the paradigmatic representative of this attitude, the Nietzsche of *The Will to Power*, who set out his famous criticism of the connection between responsibility and free will, a connection postulated according to him by theologians with the aim of making humanity dependent on them: "men have been considered 'free' in order to be judged and sentenced, in order to be guilty" (*Twilight of the Idols*, Oxford: Oxford World Classics, 1998, p. 31).

4. Hans Magnus Enzensberger, *Civil War* (London: Granta Books, 1994). A sharp theoretical — almost methodological, I would go so far as to say: the very category of civil war is questioned — criticism is the one

presented by Alessandro Dal Lago in his note "Enzesberger l'apocalittico" (*Micromega*, no. 5/94, November–December 1994), 129–34.

5. For a sharp and detailed analysis of the economic transformations that have given rise to this ideological and cultural phenomenon called postmodernity, see David Harvey's book *The Condition of Postmodernity* (Oxford: Basil Blackwell, 1989). The hypothesis of the work is that there is a certain kind of necessary relation among the appearance of postmodern cultural forms, the emergence of more flexible modes of accumulation of capital and a new cycle of what the author calls "space/time compression" in the organization of capitalism.

6. See his *Reasons and Persons* (Oxford: Clarendon Press, 1984).

7. Hannah Arendt, in *Entre historia y acción*, Paidós. Similar statements are to be found in *The Human Condition* (Chicago: University of Chicago Press, 1958) especially the last part of chapter 5, concerned with action.

8. Hans Jonas, *The Imperative of Responsibility: In Search of Ethics for the Technological Age* (translation of *Das Prinzip Verantwortung*), translated by Hans Jonas and David Herr (Chicago: University of Chicago Press, 1984), p. 4.

9. *The Imperative of Responsibility*, cit., p. 7.

10. *Entre historia y acción*.

11. "It is in the nature of beginning that something new is started which cannot be expected from whatever may have happened before." *The Human Condition*, cit., p. 177.

12. *The Human Condition*, cit., p. 178.

13. *The Human Condition*, cit., p. 176.

14. Jonas's actual words are: "The object of *responsibility* is emphatically the perishable *qua* perishable [. . .] this far from perfect object, entirely contingent *in* its facticity, perceived precisely in its perishability, indigence and insecurity, must have the power to move me through its sheer existence (not through special qualities) to place my person at its service, free of all appetite for appropriation" (*The Imperative of Responsibility*, cit., p. 87) See also the work by Jean Greisch, "L'amour du monde et le principe de responsabilité," in Monette Vacquin (ed.), *La responsabilité* (Paris: Éditions Autrement, 1994), especially pp. 82 et seq.

15. *The Imperative of Responsibility*, cit., p. 28.

16. Arendt put this message into the mouths of (then) imaginary parents, addressed to their children: "In this world even we are not very securely at home: how to move about in it, what to know, what skills to master, are mysteries to us too. You must try to make out as best you can; in any case you are not entitled to call us to account. We are innocent, we wash our hands of you." The way she disqualifies them could not be more categorical: "Anyone who refuses to assume joint responsibility for the world should not have children *and must not be allowed to take part in educating them*" (my emphasis) (*Between Past and Future: Eight Exercises in Political Thought,* London: Penguin Books, 1985, 1st ed. 1961, pp. 191 and 189). The quotations are taken from the work "The Crisis in Education."

17. Pascal Bruckner has also referred to this in his book *The Temptation of Innocence* (New York: Algora Publishing, 2000), in which, as one of the most characteristic tendencies of modern society in addition to victimization, he points to infantilism.

18. As opposed to what it might seem at first glance, this is not a gratuitous supposition. See the article by Arendt, "Reflections on Little Rock," *Dissent*, vol. 6, no. 1, 46–56 (republished in *Public Life: A Journal of Politics*, vol. 4, no. 3/4, May–June 1973).

19. *The Imperative of Responsibility*, cit., p. 345.

20. "The only strictly utopian element in Marx's teachings" is "the emancipation of man from labor . . . Emancipation from labor is emancipation from necessity" (*The Human Condition*, cit. pp. 130–1).

21. G. Even-Granboulan, "Hannah Arendt face à l'histoire" in Anne-Marie Roviello and Maurice Weyembergh (eds), *Hannah Arendt et la modernité* (Paris: Vrin, 1992), p. 80.

22. Victoria Camps has dealt with this distinction in her book *Virtudes públicas* (Madrid: Espasa Calpe, 2nd ed. 1990), especially in chapter 3, devoted to responsibility, which includes a section entitled "La responsabilidad sin culpa." For my own part I have written down some thoughts on this matter in my book *¿A quién pertenece lo ocurrido?* (Madrid: Taurus, 1995), in particular in section 7.3 entitled "¿Responsabilidad o culpabilidad?"

23. So that "what has once begun takes the law of action out of our hands, and the accomplished facts, created by the beginning, become cumulatively

the law of its continuation" (*The Imperative of Responsibility*, cit., p. 32).

24. I had expressly defended this thesis in my book *Narratividad: la nueva síntesis* (Barcelona: Península, 1986) and I returned to the subject in *Filosofía de la Historia* (Barcelona: Paidós, 1991), especially in "Epílogo. Reconsideración a la baja del sujeto," pp. 165–86.

CHAPTER 2

Toward an Innocent Responsibility

1. Elsewhere[1] I had already begun to deal with the subject I would now like to return to from a different perspective. I must mention, not only as a courtesy to the readers of those papers (although I am well aware that their numbers are small, but I have to be pleasant to all of them because they are mostly friends), but also primarily as a presumably methodological argument that excuses, or at least helps to excuse, the overt, interested bias I want to give the subject of responsibility on this occasion.

That does not mean that I am turning my back on my own statements, that I would like to wipe the slate of my thought clean, or anything of the sort. To bear witness to that I will take, as a theoretical starting motif, an acute observation made to me recently by Carlos Moya[2] in a personal note. To my doubtless emphatic formulation (from *¿A quién pertenece lo ocurrido?*) "we are responsible for what we have the capacity to do," he sensibly retorted with the example "I have the capacity to insult someone (and many other things), but if I do not insult him, I am not responsible for insulting him."

I have to begin by acknowledging that my formulation should have been more qualified. Perhaps what I was trying to point out would have been clearer if I had said, for example, "responsibility must be measured *in relation to* capacity" or "everyone is responsible *in relation to* what it is in his power to do." It would then have been easier to see both that the question I was trying to put was connected with what in the traditional terminology of this discourse are usually called *actions by omission* (the only actions in which someone can be imputed precisely for not having done something he should have or was expected of him, where it makes sense to say that someone is responsible for nothing happening) and that I was trying to incorporate an order of prior considerations that are not used often in these concepts. There are, to put it in a nutshell, *spheres of imputability* that configure and constitute the link of responsibility.

To talk as if there were only actions, on the one hand, and individuals to which they can be attributed, on the other, is to sketch a scenario which starts from an equality among agents that is not the case, an equality that is barely attenuated by the fact that we can then introduce, as a kind of backdrop, conditions or conditioning factors. But it is also a way of trying to avoid outside interference, of looking for what we might call spaces of irresponsibility (which in some cases may be of moral impunity). A sphere in which this is demonstrated in exemplary fashion is that of political battles, in which it is common to argue as if responsibility were exclusive to those who hold (or have held) power. Of course, I am not denying that most of that load must be borne by those who occupy (or have occupied) the highest levels of political decision making. But neither power nor responsibility end there. Living in the palace cannot be the criterion. The executive does not mark the boundaries of power, nor do the accounts governments periodically have to render in democracy cancel all responsibilities. Just a note, which I will take up again later: by accepting this thesis, someone who never knew victory (in whatever sphere) would never be responsible for anything. Which, by definition, would doom a question that is neither trivial nor indifferent to remaining unanswered: is anyone responsible in defeats? (A question the perhaps excessively grave tones of which could be softened if it were reformulated as, in what sense are those who lost mistaken?)

The point is not, of course, to combat those different attempts at exclusion by opposing an indiscriminate universalization of the link (of responsibility). Rather, the idea here is that the best way of combating the *we are all responsible* argument, a traditionally conservative one insofar as it sets out to defuse any criticism of power by smashing it to smithereens,[3] is not by launching an insipid *responsibility is the virtue of the sad* (or any other thesis of similar inspiration), but by trying to show properly how the concept fits the consequences deriving from it. One effective approach to the analysis might be to try to show the elements that constitute it.

The question of responsibility, it has been said more than once, can be broken down into several sub-questions, each of which points to a clearly differentiated development. However, it is true that there can be no complete elucidation of responsibility in a particular situation unless we can answer the following questions: Who is responsible? What are they responsible for? To whom are they responsible? In the name of what are they responsible? A complete elucidation so much demands an answer to all the questions that the dismissal of any of them as pertinent ruins the very possibility of tackling the more general issue. It makes no sense to allot responsibility for a random event (because there is no *who* it depends on), just as there is no crime without a *corpus delicti* (here the *what* is missing) or that it is not appropriate to demand responsibility from a hermit or Robinson Crusoe (who have no *whom* to answer to), nor, lastly, is it interesting to discover who is responsible for something lacking in any value (*in the name of what?*).

Now, having established the necessary interconnection among the different questions, we must add that that is no reason why the way we deal with each of the answers has to be the same. So the question about the *who* stirs up a whole set of problems about the need for the subjective entity as such. As has been pointed out all too often, there is little element of chance in the coincidence between critics (and criticism) of subjectivity and critics (and criticism) of responsibility. Once the subject has been deactivated, declared obvious, unnecessary, superfluous or, worse still, a mere interested phantasmagoria (shifting Chinese shadows emerging from the hands of the powerful), keeping up the effort to locate people responsible can only be a final maneuver by that power to produce subjects and subjected in a single gesture, since what would make them apparently autonomous and self-sufficient entities would be what at the same time, through the guilt mechanism — which according to them constitutes responsibility — would make them absolutely docile.[4] For its part the matter of the interrogator, the one demanding an answer, sooner or later refers through intersubjectivity to the sphere where the interrogation takes place; that is the sphere of what is common, what is shared, the social sphere in short, which is where the demand for responsibility is made. Thirdly, the question about the values contained in it (in the name of what?) refers most of all to a discussion about codes and discourses (moral or legal), which is not the one I want to raise now.

The apparently simplest question is left for the end, the one that seems to be answered with the mere establishment of its object: what are they responsible for? There would be a first reply that, at least at a glance, seems to clearly point out the place where we have to keep looking: someone is responsible for what is done. The problem — the father and mother of all problems, in fact — is that such an answer refers to a series of far more general considerations about the nature of action, the content attributed to that act. A vital initial qualification had already been made when talking of *actions by omission*: we shall have to understand *doing* in a sufficiently broad sense for it to include *not-doing* in certain conditions.

The importance of the nuance is related to the transcendence that actions of this kind have been acquiring in recent times. The disturbing hypothesis that they have become the figure that best allows us to visualize the relation men in the world today have with their own acts is worth taking into account, even if only because consequences of many different kinds follow from its acceptance or rejection. It is clear that at the root of the idea of omission, providing its foundations, there is another idea that should be made explicit: that there is a course of events that, without the intervention of human action, tends to its consummation. That, of course, had already appeared in the traditional formulations of this subject. When the usual example of the obligation to help in the event of a car accident is brought out, it is being taken for granted that a refusal of help (*action by omission* in this case) is not indifferent, since it produces its own effects (it is likely that the situation of the people injured in the accident will worsen if they are not given immediate assistance etc). Note, by the way, that situations of this kind allow us to show to what extent the identification of responsibility with guilt, above and beyond any basic doctrinal discrepancies,[5] is not technically operative in all contexts. Moya's reproach mentioned at the beginning of the chapter functioned on the basis of the identification between both categories, so that one could not quite see what could be asked of the person who does not insult. In situations of this kind — the kind that has tended to be taken as a model so far — the feature was that there was an *outside* to the action, characterized by its indifference. But if, on the contrary, we think of the example of assistance, then there is no indifferent option — in other words, no irresponsible option. The person who does not stop to help is responsible (with the connotation of guilt) for that negative action, while the one who does is responsible (this time in the sense that he has the right to be attributed the merit) for the help provided.

But the limitations of that identification do not end here. For it to function there is a requirement that greatly reduces its territory of application. There can only be responsibility, understood as guilt, for actions already performed.

However, these are not the only kind we need to speak of. Our projects, desires or aspirations also come fully within the sphere (under the rubric *possible actions*), though that categorization cannot be used. By definition, it is not appropriate to start looking for people to blame for what is still to be done, but it makes perfect sense, despite the inevitable ignorance, to assign responsibility. That is the case when we say things like "parents are responsible for the education of their children." What we are saying is that it is up to them to take charge of it, regardless of how the process turns out in the end. More generally, the statement "you will be responsible for what may happen" makes perfect sense, whereas its correlate, "you will be to blame for what may happen," makes none, or at least not clearly (unless we give some non-ironic meaning to expressions like *to be to blame for an unfortunate incident*).

2. Now, to return to the beginning, to propose actions by omission as a *figure of reference* implies a certain review of the approaches the discourse of action of the analytic tradition had been taking toward its object. In this debate — as in so many more in the history of thought, but that is beside the point now — problems are often posed not so much because some people do not know or do not take notice of what others say as because they do not give them the importance the others attribute to them. If we do not want to enter directly into this argument yet, we could propose another example to keep us amused until the time comes.

The argument over different philosophical paradigms when dealing with the subject of action frequently focuses on a clarification of what kind of action is the model that enlightens human acts as such. The supporters of not very rationalist philosophies stress the importance of factors such as desire, passion, feelings etc, and consequently tend to focus their attention on those moments or episodes when individuals are swept along by them, while the authors who have not abandoned the gnoseological horizon of scientific values emphasize the fact that the really important actions are the ones that can be understood rationally, explicitly or implicitly, and the other factors must be relegated to the category of a mere insignificant accompaniment to the act — and therefore the actions they could lead to are irrelevant events. We shall observe that this is a *goal* or principle argument, which does not allow for being resolved with any of the particular criteria involved. The rational justification of rationality, like the passionate defense of passion, is as easy as it is useless because it is a tautology. The question is quite another one — that is, of quite another nature. To argue that we should take actions by omission as a *primordial example* (a formulation that is only slightly distant from what we have been calling a model or figure) alters, I would go so far as to say radically, the balance among the theoretical elements present. The argument no longer revolves around the agent — whether to reaffirm him or to subvert him — and shifts to a sphere that is different and is, of course, greater. The former player loses his condition as a privileged territory where the most important part of the action takes place and takes on a subordinate one, subsidiary to the new space where things happen. Now it is he who must find his insertion in or accommodation to a reality where the fundamental things are given — that is, already charged with significance (and not made significant for him).[6]

It should of course be argued that the significance the agent finds is, in turn, the result of previous human actions. However, such an argument does not alter the datum of experience about the way in which agents tend to live their insertion in reality. But more important than that is the fact that we are not looking at a mere effect of ignorance, like the one described by the old theory of the ideologies in the Marxist tradition. It is not a matter of men not recognizing what is their own, what they themselves have produced, and becoming confused when they try to reify that estrangement. It is rather that the reality they have to face is increasingly configured, standardized, programmed in its development, thanks to the efficacy of global entities that operate in scenarios outside the control of any particular agents.

There would be little theoretical interest in entering into this to try to reproduce arguments, which are out of date by now anyway, such as the room for intervention individuals have with structures, or any of the many equivalents. But we must add immediately that it would be as ridiculous as discovering the Mediterranean little by little to refuse on principle (as if the idea — from Ecclesiastes, in fact — that there could be something new under the sun were still capable of generating perplexity) to admit that the transformations that are taking place at breakneck speed in our societies oblige us to reconsider many of the theoretical schemas we have operated with so far. From several spheres we have received signals along the same lines: call it globalization, planetarization or whatever you like, the fact is that we are witnessing changes that only partially allow us to think with the old categories. Reality has expanded and contracted at the same time and in the same movement. Perhaps that is why some of the traditional spatial metaphors in which we were so comfortably settled have passed their sell-by date. What we might call the closing of the world implies that there is no longer an *outside* for this reality.

But at the same time that phenomenon of closing is what gives rise to a new opening, an opening that has to be visualized in another light, perhaps that of an opening *inward*. The possibility to be demanded now is not the find, the discovery or the conquest, but the unfulfilled promise, the defeated aspirations. Everything is there as — we know now — it always was. Awaiting agents who are capable of activating its secret purposes. But I would like this to sound not only like Benjamin (or Horkheimer) but also like Wittgenstein. A very particular Wittgenstein (the best, in my opinion), the one who knew that knowledge takes place at the moment when we are capable of perceiving what had always been before our eyes.

Tugging on some of the threads woven so far, it would not be difficult to lead this idea toward a reconsideration of historical discourse. That is not the primordial goal now, although I cannot help looking at it sympathetically (it serves, among other things, to test the theoretical scope of the issues we are dealing with). Indeed, what we have just said could be understood to be tantamount to proposing the discovery of the virtualities of the past as the primordial task for thought today. To highlight the importance of the consequences of the action symmetrically implies introducing into the idea of future[7] an element of indeterminateness through which the question of meaning can be reintroduced with full justification. Nevertheless, and although we are not going to pause here, we should not pass over the philosophical dimension (the philosophy of history, naturally) of something that had previously been elided through a question (is anyone responsible in defeats?).

The insistence of so many analysts of action on the importance of what has been done, actually carried out, seems to have various kinds of mentalism as an express polemical referent. The point, it is usually argued, is to emphasize the positive dimension of the action to avoid all those dualisms that throughout history have proved incapable of withstanding the pounding of the spiritualist temptation. But there is something in that rhetorical gesture that recalls, if I am allowed the speculative pirouette, that *metaphysical violence* that Vattimo so loves to talk about.[8] Those actions frozen in acts have a strong, suspiciously strong, ontological status. They are the new *what there is* awaiting the right discursive apparel. Beside them nothing is comparable. Anything other than that narrow *adjust to what is given* is dismissed with various reproaches that seem to conceal a single fear: if we open the floodgates of discourse to other modalities of acting, there will be no way of containing the new elements awaiting thought with which we shall be inundated.

But however justified it may be, fear does not make an abusive cutback right. Especially because the supposed solution may give rise to an even more serious difficulty than the one we are trying to avoid. The acceptance of what really happened as the only valid ontological referent becomes, if we continue to think of historical discourse, a concealed rehabilitation of a view of the past that has been thoroughly criticized by philosophers — the one that reconstructs history from the point of view of the powerful. That is where exclusive attention to what was actually the case leads. Inevitably, no thought is given to what never managed to be, what obtained no more ontological status than the unfulfilled promise, the defeated aspiration or, in short, the frustrated hope.[9] Which shows at least that the tendency to look at the past through the eyes of those who did accomplish their goals is too powerful and too encrusted in our way of approaching history to be sure that the mere antidote of an awareness of its dangers is enough to neutralize it.

But that is not the end of the advantages of changing the model for action — or primordial example, as we have also called it — although it is no small thing that they help to show some of the suppositions on which certain philosophies of action seem to rest. Perhaps more important than that is the new theoretical framework sketched out by the situations where omission is an inevitable option, and the possibility opened up by that framework of incorporating into the centrality of the discourse — its hard core, as other kinds of jargon put it — subjects that tended to be moved to the periphery of the problem, if not directly treated as anomalies. I am thinking in particular of two issues, the one related to the magnitude of the actions and the other to their consequences.

3. At bottom, it is not too difficult to see that both issues are deeply interconnected. It was an individualistic conception of subjectivity that found it

difficult to move from that sphere to other, broader ones. Whoever tends to be more reticent to accept any reality in the strong sense other than that of particular individuals will tend to doubt the existence of something like collective action (unless it is reduced to a mere appendage or juxtaposition of individual actions), and of course will judge the idea of anything like collective responsibility to be a manifest abuse of language. From here, raising the subject of consequences, and particularly unwanted consequences or perverse effects, may serve to emphasize the contingent dimension of human action, the limits of the agent or the inevitable presence of chance in any predictions we may wish to make, but in no event will it be useful for showing any necessary, structural dimension of the action.

In a way, what is being proposed here is to invert the burden of proof, to begin the discursive journey at another point, not regarding the question of the ontological status of certain entities, for example supraindividual ones, as the one to be elucidated first. Marx (it is worth remembering from time to time that he existed) adopted a similar attitude when he refused to take the concept of population as the starting point for his discourse. Similarly, and with all due respect, the point would be to shun certain approaches (not because they are nonexistent but because they are inappropriate) and, in their place, begin to tug the thread of the agents' insertion in certain situations, the ones in which, to put it in a nutshell, there are no dead ends, irrelevant possibilities that lead to a hypothetical exterior of the action.

We might speak of a *figure of the figure*, an image that visualizes that transformation in the world panorama that different categories have tried to name, each in its own way: the occupation of the planet. There is one history that, much as some people may dislike it (in view of the furore kicked up by Fukuyama it seems there are many of them), has ended beyond any doubt — that is, geographical or territorial history.[10] The occupation of the planet has, indeed, concluded. From that discovery, which is difficult to dispute, we can draw different conclusions. We may conclude that there is no longer anywhere to escape to — a Romantic expectation that in recent authors still maintained some virtuality transferred to the plane of thought in another guise — or we may conclude that the new reality makes obvious something we have known for ages but which was half hidden, concealed by appearances; in other words, the only true adventures left are the interior ones (even when they take place in natural settings). To bring the figure into the terms of the present discourse: we now see that human action necessarily turns in on itself.

Perhaps the tones, an involuntary (for me) family resemblance with other discourses that are close in time or the fact that it is common to infer identification from a simple mention, could lead someone to think that in the end what is being proposed here is one more variant of those ideas for weakening subjectivity that end up having the simultaneous weakening of the idea of responsibility as an inevitable theoretical effect. To understand something in that way would be to misinterpret what has been said — that is, to locate it in a discourse schema that does not concern it. The problem is not (it probably never was) strengthening the subject the better to defend responsibility or, the other way round, attacking it to make it impossible. To put it that way excludes thinking about what really matters now — that is, the specific link the agent maintains with his action and that we call responsibility. Now that we have reached this point, everything we have said so far about the new configuration of the world should serve to pin down the idea of responsibility we are defending and, incidentally, the distances that separate it from other uses of the same idea. For, indeed, it cannot be said that the tendency of thought in recent times has been a definitive abandoning of the category but, rather, its gradual theoretical defense[11] and its increasingly generalized use in different kinds of discourse. But it is this apparent resurgence that must force us to take all precautions. For to take many of the uses it is easy to find, for example in the media, as theoretically unchallengeable, would drag us into the mire of conceptual confusion.

So as not to abandon that distant initial example, let us think of the exchange of accusations we frequently find in political debate. Some throw in the others' faces the argument that they must take responsibility for a particular episode (usually disgraceful), to which the others reply by calling their accusers irresponsible for having made the accusation (for example, with the argument that it affects national security). It is obvious that the first group are using responsibility as a synonym for blame, and so it will not be necessary to repeat what we said at the beginning. The second group, on the other hand, are using it in a way worth commenting on.

In this second case "being responsible" could be replaced by an expression like "being prudent." Responsibility would then mean a way of determining, picking out what we are capable of handling from what is possible. Someone would be responsible insofar as he was capable of realizing how many events he is in a position to take charge of at each moment. Let us say it now: in an interpretation like this the concept lacks all tension. For even though the aim was to connect these events with possibility, the possibility that such a way of looking would be, no pun intended, a *possibilist possibility*. And it is very doubtful whether an agent who acts in that way, who assumes what he must, what is right and proper, is in any true sense responsible.

It may be just coincidence, but another context in which the adjective is used in the same way clearly has to do with the exercise of authority. When parents or teachers describe a child as responsible, they often mean something more than merely obedient. It is one step up from there: he has interiorized the rules so well that he knows what he has to do at every moment. Is this use of the category acceptable? In view of the premises we have been talking about so far, obviously not. In fact, when one analyzes it with a little care, the child in the example is perfectly irresponsible. He restricts himself to being the terminal for a rule — moral, disciplinary or of some kind — to efficiently carrying out the order he is given from above.

But following the logic of the argument, everything that identifies the practice of responsibility with the application of any rule is equally irre-sponsible. That is not the respond referred to in the etymology of the term responsibility: that is just providing the voice. It could well be said that in the end it is contradictory to speak of *necessary responsibility*. For when someone, in social life for example, is regarded as *necessarily responsible*, by the same rule a subsidiary responsible person ends up being created. Which seems to prove the relative indifference of the first one chosen, whose real function was to occupy a space, perform a function (normally undertaking to repair the possible damage of any action).

It will escape no one that a rejection of the very idea of necessary respon-sibility seems to lead us to some variant of the defense of a free responsibility. But now too we should hold back the appearance of a new concept (that of freedom), in case stating it at the beginning, as if it were the first word to be elucidated, returned us to an old circular design of the question (which can be exemplified by the hackneyed dilemma of whether man is free or prede-termined), whose scant efficacy is more than accredited. The neopositivists may not be wrong about everything: often the exaggerated antiquity of a way of posing questions is the best testimony to their sterility. Although it is also necessary to exaggerate: freedom may well be a good last word. One of those categories that are only defined after all the arguments have been deployed; one of those ideas that are usually called on after formulae like "in short, all that is what we call freedom."

4. Indeed, a rejection of that idea of responsibility should lead us to another way of understanding the terms in question. We have argued so far against different fixative, reifying, essentialist interpretations of the leading elements of this relation; against an untouchable action, once it has been performed, and against an agent who has become a mere conveyor belt for orders. But what has been rejected does not yet allow us to clearly identify the new referent of the proposal (hence the warnings against possibilism). This may well be the moment to supply those earlier allusions about the need to broaden the territory of action with more content. With the elements provided we have warned of the consequences of making do with a suspiciously modest version of possibility. In the end that interpretation, as happened with the conception of action that was too submissive to what had been done, remains the prisoner of an unacceptable philosophical vision.

To submit (a verb some people prefer to replace with *accept*) to the facts or to submit to the rules are ways, equivalent in their results, of making responsibility impossible or, rather, deactivating it, shifting it toward a sphere where it can no longer fulfill its proper function. Positivism and possibilism rob the agent at the moment when a radically understood responsibility begins to be thinkable — that is, the moment of decision. The identification of the two "–isms" is not abusive. In the end, those who restrict themselves to simply defending the possibilities that never came to anything in the past avoid asking the question of what the genuine possibilities (i.e. the impossibilities) of the present are. To settle for trying to do what could not be done at the time is to betray the nerve of that hope. In the end it is to trust that the story will end some day, the very day when the last debt will be settled, the last outstanding bill paid.

A major confusion, to be sure. The part of the past that remains unfulfilled is not the specific demand, the particular desire that can now be satisfied without difficulty. Wittgenstein was right here too: man has a tendency to rage against limits (not only of language). When all is said and done, the history of humanity is no more than the story of the formidable task of explaining the confines of experience, making the boundaries of the world grow.[12] No one can predetermine what we shall never manage to say, just as no one can know for certain what we are doomed to be unable to do. What we do have the right to suspect (Marx casts a long shadow) is the fact that man proposing something is an indicator of its possibility, but of a radical possibility — that is, a possibility that appears as desirable as it is unattainable to its contemporaries. In a nutshell, as an impossible possibility. That is what seems to be the question: a specular tension between the two terms that are attracted as often as they are repelled.[13] A tension in which the suspension of either of them would be tantamount to cutting off the path of action (the *feasible* possibility dissolves within a set time into the real, just as an impossibility with no determination whatsoever is metaphysical: pure exteriority, alienated abstraction, for which we should never ask responsibility).

Possibility, then, is not past, it is simply postponed or delayed. Rather than possibility, it is a reality awaiting materialization. If it can be argued that a commitment to the possible ends up exploding reality from within, it is on condition that we assume, as far as we are capable of thinking, the open, indeterminate character of human action. The *impossible possibility* we mentioned does not allude to a natural limit of what we can propose, nor to a hazy (and equally metaphysical) *wish-for-something-or-other*. What broadens our horizon, what really brings us up against the limits of impossibility, is the shape the process of human action has taken in the world today — the fact that one of the constitutive features of that process is exceeding itself, constantly generating conditions that make a conclusive analysis of the action impossible in terms of a mere recognition of the original project.

In a relatively recent past that interpretation of human action as a systematic generation of uncertainty was often placed at the service of a highly questionable thesis. The argument ran: striving to discover social reality as reliably as possible with the aim of transforming it better is a useless endeavor. We are like sorcerers' apprentices who unleash forces that, once activated, are completely outside our control. Conclusion: let us resign ourselves theoretically to smaller, less ambitious forms of spiritual apprehension of the world (what else were we being told about history in *The Poverty of Historicism*?), and apply ourselves in practice to fixing the small flaws that can occur on the surface of what exists, abandoning the pretension, as illusory as it is dangerous, to changing reality completely; the desire to transform the whole often leads to totalitarianism was usually the final point of this argument.

That the thesis admits openly conservative uses seems beyond any doubt. (A mere look at some of its most fervent defenders provides a fairly unambiguous initial clue.) But it would be ridiculous to refuse to accept an argument that is consistent in itself for the sole reason that it is part of a wider idea with which we are in global disagreement. The comparison with the sorcerer's apprentice is not entirely mistaken: it may be insufficient. And somewhat defeatist. To lay down that no action obtains the result its agent proposed helps to promote a derationalized image of the sphere of human action (since what defines that unruly effect is not its integration in another order of intelligibility but the mere fact that it departs from the program, operates aside from any purpose).

It may well have been the danger of the paradox becoming a contradiction that led the authors who posed this problem for the first time to sideline it. Their attitude was natural: to place it at the center would have meant disdaining the function knowledge has performed throughout history; its mission has always been to warn man about the threats of the future. To pose the loss of meaning of the action itself, and the deadly distancing of the product from the purpose, as inevitable would require a complementary theory to account for the reasons for that *constitutive slowness* that encumbers knowledge of humanity and prevents it from ever reaching its object, which, from a similar perspective, would always be two or three effects ahead of the discourse that aims to apprehend it.

The differential nuance between this last approach and the one we are trying to propose now has to do with that reference to the form the process of human action has taken, which we mentioned before. That reference alluded not only to the processes of globalization and planetarization, with their element of (tentative) closure of reality, but also, and this is what is to be added now, the new function knowledge has started to perform. The unwanted effects no longer have to do solely with a generic complexity of reality, nor exclusively with the inevitable conflict caused by the collusion of free intentional individual actions. It is knowledge itself that, when it becomes one more productive force, is contributing to multiply the effects of the action in previously unthinkable magnitudes. The process of setting knowledge in general (and science in particular) in economic activity and social life has led to a situation where the agent is obliged to constantly reconsider what the suitable scales are. And so in the sectors where technological development has reached a high level (the computer or telecommunications industries, for instance) the efficacy of the positive or negative consequences of knowledge has no precedent in previous human history. We might say that those forced nineteenth-century fantasies about the dangers and virtues of science now hang from a thread, the same thread from which our confidence in, or our fear, of the future hangs.

(For years, with slight variations, the Hollywood industry offered us the same story that seemed to be a parable for our dizzy perplexity about knowledge. It is the story of the teenager who, with the simple aid of his technical skill and mental agility, gets inside the computer system of some multinational organization or state apparatus. The turn the story took, the darker or lighter tone, depended on the director's assessment of the lightning advances of computer technology. The novelty of this hardly imaginary situation, what allows us to recognize ourselves in the story, may well be that particular combination of fear of the unwanted consequences of our own actions and awareness of the extreme fragility of our knowledge, since it no longer seems to be visualized in the figure of a fortress — there is no need to be a doctor or be called Frankenstein or Mengele to do outrageous things — but, rather, an open place, densely populated and with no protection whatsoever.)

The point is not to oppose a qualitative perspective to a quantitative one, as if it were a matter of before and now. It is more to show the way margins of indeterminacy or uncertainty, which in the past could be reabsorbed by later actions (the trusting *there is a solution for everything*), now seem irreversible. In fact, if we think about it for a moment, we are warned of this tendency, just that one of the specific possible effects, the most terrifying (the hypothetical final disaster) may well have clouded our attention and prevented us from a pondered global analysis. But in the end what underlay so many apocalyptic discourses that reached their splendor in the late 1970s and early 1980s was the conviction that it is impossible to forget what we know, the certainty that knowledge had reached a point where the effects of any action that used it were projected to infinity.

By establishing all that, we are doing something more — albeit only a little more — than merely pointing out that the possibility is being deployed (and displayed) in history. We are saying that in all that matters *it is man who generates his own impossibility*, that impossibility he will later confront. Hence the earlier reservation about the metaphor of the sorcerer's apprentice who steps back in terror from the forces he has clumsily unleashed. It might be more in accordance with what we have said to compare the man who strives to realize the possible with the one who chases his own shadow, provided the new comparison is not understood, like the myth of Sisyphus, as a frustrating and repetitive confrontation with a reality that tirelessly defeats all comers, but as an endless, but not meaningless, process. A process in which (for all the shadow always remains beyond, doomed to exteriority) the ground it occupied is won by the pursuer, who thus acquires awareness that if there has to be an end to the chase it can only be reconciliation, or recognition that it was an estranged, repressed or alienated dimension of himself that he was fighting to catch up with. And although trying to squeeze more out of a metaphor than one should is always a delicate exercise (and a dangerous point: we already know that the ruin of the example usually involves the ruin of the exemplified), we should add that, for all it may be a matter of pursuing something that was always ours, the place where we finally catch up with the shadow is an *objective* place, regarding which there is at least one possible decision. That is, whether we run in the right direction or abstain from any initiative and spend our time waiting for reality to present us with the coincidence at some time or other.

5. Responsibility, then? Or better still, responsibility, still? Yes, just in another way and possibly in another place. It would at least be strange after all we have said to continue to defend a conception of the thing in which the old emphases were not altered. For example, it seems difficult to keep talking, as if it were an operative determination, about responsibility for action in terms of responsibility for its effects. But it seems less so to accept that when action bursts its own bounds we should reconsider the content of old notions like collective action. For if, indeed, that agent's loss of authority, as we will call it, over his own act that we referred to earlier is written in the new nature of the process, we shall have to begin to think about whether that is not giving rise to a new kind of collective action, the result of the confluence of the unwanted effects of individual intentional actions.

This new collective action — heterogeneous, primitive, anonymous in a way — is to a large extent the new referent responsibility must be related to.

Of course, there were always collective actions; by definition the individual cannot be presented with the bills of history. What has changed is the relation between them and their protagonists. We should therefore wonder about the reason why, being perfectly aware of the collective nature of certain historical or social processes, a large number of contemporary thinkers are reluctant to admit the existence of actions of that type. The answer can be guessed at without too much difficulty: it is the doubts about the existence today of that possible collective subject in a position to take charge of the action on that scale that fundamentally explain their reluctance.

Of course, there are counterarguments to this position. We should not dwell too long on them because this is not basically the discussion that matters now. We could advance ideas of the *actions in search of an author* kind, for example, or emphasize that the existence of protagonists on the necessary scale is almost a condition of possibility for making certain episodes in human reality intelligible. But since this is an interesting point, it would oblige us to reopen a kind of debate that would divert us from our goal at this moment. To that end it will be better to keep only what is indicative about the reticent position in the face of the idea of the collective subject. Indicative of the dissolution, of the deterioration of certain forms of social cohesion that once not only provided individuals with a well-defined feeling of belonging to a suprasubjective entity on a larger scale but also created the material conditions for that suprasubjective entity to assume particular actions as its own.

But this is just to sketch a framework, to draw the space where the issue must be approached. The specific question this section opened with is still posed in almost the same terms: do these actions *where the protagonist is dubious* oblige us to reformulate the subject of responsibility? Or, to take one more step, does our perplexity over them tell us of some specific characteristic in the light of which the subject should be considered now? I think so. In fact, to insist on the character of any kind of collective subject as a construction with the aim of weakening it ontologically is to be sidetracked (to put it perhaps too categorically: is the individual subject not also a construction?). The central issue is another. It is not so much that we do not know how to find the protagonists of these new actions as that we fail to find an essential moment in their behavior.

It might be fairer to formulate the issue by stating that what is difficult to find in these actions is the moment of decision.[14] Or, rather, what is extremely problematic is the existence of collective decisions. Immediately after writing this one can imagine the critical reader ready to ask: "but were there ever decisions of this kind at any time in the past?" Unless we misinterpret the content of the expression "collective decision" we can answer yes. The point, of course, is not to talk as if somewhere in the past there was some kind of ideal communication community, capable of talking through an agreement on common goals and actions to be taken.[15] The point is whether, through procedures for taking decisions agreed intersubjectively, the agents who have to argue for and carry out certain actions visualize the moment when the decision is taken wherever it may be, so that the moment after it is accepted or rejected it becomes possible. (The theoreticians of democracy could have some relevant things to say about this.)

That is exactly what seems to be in question. It is this blurring of the foundational moment of the decision that most confuses us when thinking about the way we must consider responsibility today. Now we can see that the usual language of intentionality was to some extent an insufficient one, or an insufficiently fine-tuned one for thinking about this matter. The big moment, the moment when the agent establishes an important link with the action, is the one when he has to decide. We could also say, if you prefer, that that is the moment of commitment. Perhaps we cannot go much further than this when it comes to demanding responsibilities, but it is no small thing. For the decision calls for its fulfillment, requires its performance. So that there is something of a failed, frustrated, stillborn action about a decision that is not carried out. Indeed, the connotations with which we use the terms in our ordinary language reinforce that interpretation. We usually dismiss anyone who takes decisions and then fails to follow through as *indecisive*. Whereas we call the person who goes ahead, who does what he decided to do, *determined*.

Although the term "commitment" we have just introduced conjures up some rather outdated philosophies, it might still be able to do us some belated service for the purposes of referring to that particular nexus the agent establishes with his action when he decides. Indeed, unlike the term "intention," the decision is binding and demands precision. It comes as no surprise that someone should express diffuse, vague, almost unidentifiable intentions. We often find the term "intention" adorned with adjectives like "dark" or "dishonorable," as if hinting that the intentional allows for degrees of reality and visibility. And so, without requiring specifications, we can accept a statement of the "I have every intention of changing my life" variety. However, we find that same language totally unacceptable when we are talking about a decision. So much so that, if someone were to try it, we would immediately ask them to be more specific. In this second case, if the imaginary interlocutor of a moment ago were to change the terms of his statement and say, "I have decided to change my life," almost without stopping to think we would ask him something like "and what will that change consist of?" taking it for granted that he has something specific in mind. And if he answered, "I don't know yet" or something similar, we would tend to conclude that his ideas are not clear (or that he has not mastered the language).

As an added advantage, this shift of attention toward the moment of the decision allows us to skirt some of the recurrent problems that arose in the classical discourse of action whenever the subject of intention cropped up. Now we can begin to consider that many of those problems may well have arisen from the slippery, imprecise nature of the category itself. That makes it keep its distance, a distance that sometimes looks unbridgeable, from the action itself. The verb "intend" — let us put it to the test again in its language — is reluctant to allow itself to be conjugated in the same way as the verb "act." As some authors have pointed out,[16] "intend" has no gerund, a limitation from which some might infer an ontological feature of the intentional, something like its hesitant reality (indeed, when someone refers with retroactive effects to the moment when an intention began to take shape, in a way what he is trying to indicate, unintentionally, is his powerlessness to describe the precise nature of the process). In the face of that, the strong position in the language occupied by decision, together with what we have already pointed out, authorizes us to see it as the first face of action.

If this is the essential moment of action as development, it is the only one when the link with the agent can be spoken of without ambiguity, and there is a need to set the idea of responsibility right here. As was made manifest when it was stated, the initial insistence on distinguishing it from the idea of blame was trying to break the identification between the question of responsibility and the problem of reparation for any damage an action might have caused. With no aspiration to minting new categorizations, the distinction might be expressed by saying that one has to *answer for* one's own decision, while as far as the share of its effects are concerned, the point is *to take charge of* them.

The ambiguity of this last expression, we have to acknowledge, is deliberate. The fact that it can also be used to allude to an understanding (what happens when, as we said at the beginning, we ask someone to *"hacer cargo"* — to be aware — of our situation), the aspect of relation the category has, that dimension of *sharing out the world* I have alluded to elsewhere,[17] stands out especially when we pose the matter in terms of *attribution of responsibility*. Let me make it clear that there is no intention of disdaining that other aspect, deeply rooted in our spontaneous way of seeing things. It may well be indicative of a certain moral progress — at least if we compare it with the lukewarm "what can we do?" not to mention the unpleasant "they'll manage somehow" — our tendency to demand that someone assume the damage caused by human actions. But for the purposes of discourse it may be best not to confuse indignation with logical necessity.[18]

From what we have been saying we can see that the criterion of responsibility for an action will be the presence and quality of the decision. Which means, if we try (at least minimally) to be specific, that it will not always have to be possible to find a person responsible who fits the current reality of a particular situation. When someone, for instance, denounces — with good intentions above any suspicion — the current situation in some African country, it would be almost a variant of the naturalistic fallacy to take it for granted that the harsh reality of that situation arises from the need for the existence of someone responsible for what is happening. In a sense that reality could exemplify the collective actions we were talking about earlier, where there comes a moment when the sets of particular actions reach an autonomy and a speed that distance them irreversibly from the purposes and intentions that provided them with their initial impulse.

This idea also implies that, almost the opposite, it will make sense to speak of responsibility even though we are not capable of finding any effect that can be attributed to the action of the subject. The "Letters from Germans" included in chapter 8 of *The Drowned and the Saved* show some of the reactions to the reading of *If This Is a Man*[19] among fellow countrymen of the Nazi torturers. It would be wrong to interpret such reactions — so accurately dissected by Primo Levi — as mere manifestations of a Judaeo-Christian mentality, or in the light of categories of some variant of collective psychoanalysis. For most of Levi's correspondents do not feel guilty, if by guilt we understand, as we proposed a while ago, the way in which the subject makes certain consequences of action his own.[20] But that is not enough to make them feel they are on the margins of what has happened, as if it had nothing to do with them.

What they are all saying, expressly or tacitly, is that that reality had no exterior, that it was not possible to invoke a nondecision: in any of the cases something was being done. They are inviting us to think that the more important the action in question, the greater its historical transcendence, the more we are obliged to consider it in terms of that inexcusable action we referred to at the beginning. Making it clear that, since different effects follow from adopting one attitude or another (the supposed non-attitude of the indecisive), we should not identity this with statements of the "we are all equally responsible" variety. We shall never be so insofar as our decisions are not the same. We may be unequally responsible. What makes us equal is the inescapable moment of the decision, not its content.

Perhaps in this way and for this case the zero degree of responsibility is expressed by that feeling of shame to which some of the Germans in the book and Levi himself refer repeatedly,[21] a feeling that could be understood as the responsibility for having decided to be, to accept oneself as a citizen of a particular country, or simply for being there, for remaining in the world. At this point it is not easy to keep using the terms and their distinctions as if they were precision instruments. And so in the sphere of guilt the equivalent of that feeling of shame would be that metaphysical guilt that corresponds in the end to the fact of having survived a situation in which the very principles of coexistence have disappeared.[22]

But I would venture to argue that, rather than to any gesture of one's own, guilt is related to unease over the fact that evil exists. And although I have to confess a deep disgust at the mere possibility that it might seem as if I am using Primo Levi for philological tasks, it may be worth pointing out how he distinguishes between the two terms we have been referring to:

It was the same shame which we knew so well, which submerged us after the selections, and every time we had to witness or undergo an outrage: the shame [. . .] which the just man experiences *when confronted by a crime committed by another*, and he feels remorse because of its existence, because of its having been irrevocably introduced into the world of existing things, and because his will has proven nonexistent or feeble and was incapable of putting up a good defense.[23]

One of the conclusions that can be drawn from all this is that the expression "collective responsibility" can only be understood as the way in which subjects take part or join in a design accepted by the group, and make it their own as a collective design insofar as they recognize its scope. The same thing happens with supposed collective guilt. The only thing that might be acceptable — and for reasons of another order, which are not the case now — would be common reparation for the damage caused, but not sanction and much less punishment ("when punishment is collective it cannot be fair," Levi replied to a young Bavarian student). But such a conclusion, albeit important, may not be the one that should be emphasized in this last section.

By shifting the emphasis toward the moment of the decision, what we are basically proposing is placing the notion of responsibility in the light of the terms in the connection of which it becomes more intelligible. The decision is not well thought out from the point of view of what happened. There is no satisfactory reconstruction of that moment that does not take into account the element of indeterminacy, of risk even, with which the agent lives the tension with his project when it is no more than that. The worst part of the identification of guilt and responsibility, and the identification of both of them with reparation for the damage caused, may well be the elision of the moment that matters and beyond that the forgetting of the entity that gives meaning to the whole process. It is natural for it not to matter who takes charge of that merely reparatory responsibility; the only thing that does matter in such a case is the result. But the same cannot be said of the decision. The person who abdicates his capacity to decide is abdicating something fundamental, constitutive.[24] It is clear: those adjectives do not depend on what, but on whom. Even when there is no bet, the gambler is always in play, even when playing the strange game of losing. It is his very being that is — because he has called it — in question. The decision is the gesture with which we symbolically appropriate the future, the faint trace we try to leave on its still immaculate surface.[25] And that is what we are doomed to answer for.

Notes

1. *¿A quién pertenece lo ocurrido?*, especially in chapter 7, entitled "¿Quién ha sido?"

2. Carlos Moya is the author of, among other recent contributions to the subject of action, the perceptive introduction to the Spanish translation of various articles by Donald Davidson, *Mente, mundo y acción* (Barcelona: Paidós/ICE-UAB, 1992).

3. Although there are other ways, similar in the end, of carrying out such an operation, such as the persistent and deliberate confusion between political liberalism (which preaches the responsibility of the individual) and economic liberalism (bent on abolishing public responsibility).

4. The reader interested in this debate will find arguments in favor of the different theoretical positions in conflict in M. Cruz (ed.), *Tiempo de Subjetividad* (Barcelona: Paidós, 1996).

5. By no means minor, naturally. See here chapter 3, entitled "Responsibilidad" as it happens, of Roberto Esposito's book *Confines de lo político* (Madrid: Trotta, 1996).

6. Unless some qualification is made, summary affirmations, like categorical tones, can produce their own unwanted effect; in this case, suggesting that the attitude being described is a strict *novum* in the reflection on action. The question, as we have just pointed out, is not one of discovery but one of emphasis. But that the philosophy of action of analytic inspiration had also thought about this subject was expounded very early in Spain by Salvador Giner in his article "Intenciones humanas y estructuras sociales: aproximación crítica a la lógica situacional" (*Cuadernos Económicos de ICE*, 1977). A corrected and expanded version, with an extensive updated bibliography, is to be found under the title "Acción humana y estructura social" in M. Cruz, ed., *Acción humana* (Barcelona: Ariel, 1997). Together with this text, the most complete book available in Spanish on the situational explanation of intentional action is probably the one by Amparo Gómez, *Sobre actores y tramoyas* (Barcelona: Anthropos, 1992).

7. I shall be returning to this subject at a little more leisure in chapter 3.

8. A powerful conviction that in his latest text he has placed at the service of a *sui generis* defense of Christianity. Gianni Vattimo, *Belief* (Oxford: Polity Press, 1999). Translation of *Credere di credere* (Milan: Garzanti, 1996).

9. "History portrays everything as if it could never have come otherwise. Yet it could have happened in a hundred different ways. History is on

the side of what has happened, detaching it in a stronger context from what has not happened. Among all possibilities, it banks on the one, the surviving one. Thus history always seems as if it existed for the *stronger*, for what has actually happened; it could not have *not* happened, it *had* to happen" (Elias Canetti, *The Human Province*, translated by Joachim Neugroschel, London: André Deutsch, 1985, p. 124).

10. Daniel Brauer referred to this matter in his work "Historia y Utopía en la concepción de Kant de una paz perpetua," in the collective volume *Os 200 anos de A Paz Perpetua* (Porto Alegre: Editora da Univesidade 1995).

11. A good example of this, in sharply contrasted philosophical spheres, could be the works of Gilles Lipovetsky (in particular, *Le Crépuscule du devoir*), the frequent defenses of the ideas of Apel or even the growing interest in the figure of Hans Jonas.

12. Or to put it in the words of Max Weber in his famous lecture *The Profession of Politics*: "Certainly all historical experience confirms the truth — that man would not have attained the possible unless time and again he had reached out for the impossible."

13. See Jacques Derrida, *The Other Heading* (Bloomington and Indianapolis: Indiana University Press, 1992).

14. On this point I am indebted to Francisco Naishtat, who made some observations that were most useful for what follows, and who has written about this in "El lugar de la decisión en la acción racional: de la decisión como deseo, cálculo y acto," included in O. Nudler (comp.), *La racionalidad: su poder y sus límites* (Buenos Aires: Paidós, 1996), pp. 329–51.

15. See Jorge Dotti, "Acción humana y teoría política: la decisión," in *Acción humana*, cit., pp. 213–34, where this is posed in the light of both Arendt's and Carl Schmitt's ideas.

16. That would be the case, for example, mentioned by Naishtat (note 38), on Bergson and his immediate data of consciousness.

17. In my *¿A quién pertenece lo ocurrido?*, cit.

18. See Epilogue, "The Insomniac's Meditation."

19. Both published, together with the third of the trilogy, in *The Truce* (London: Orion Press, 1960).

20. This arises in the same way in the law when the — more objective, so to speak — question of the attribution of guilt has to be tackled. The

determination of the guilt of a subject consists of nothing more than pointing to whether or not the event of which he is accused can be attributed to him. From which, among other things, we may take it that there is nothing like guilt in itself, only guilt of the illegal event, an event that is a matter exclusively for the jury.

21. In fact, it may well be a realization that any lucid person who has lived through a similar situation must inevitably experience. Ortega wrote in 1937 from Buenos Aires, on the occasion of the death of Miguel de Unamuno: "In these months so many fellow countrymen have died that we survivors feel a strange shame at not having died as well." "En la muerte de Unamuno," *Obras completas*, V (Madrid, Revista de Occidente, 1964).

22. See Roberto Esposito, *Confines de lo político*, cit., especially pp. 57–62.

23. *The Truce*, quoted by the author in *The Drowned and the Saved* (London: Abacus, 1986), p. 54 (my emphasis).

24. Just as the person who is denied his capacity to decide when he is declared legally not responsible for his actions (for example, because his mental faculties are disturbed) is being deprived of a basic feature of himself. If, as Federico Menéndez recalled in his speech at the Conference on Discapacity held in La Coruña in Feburary 1997 at the Fundación Paideia, the legal definition of capacity is "legal suitability to enjoy a right," the denial of that capacity is tantamount to expelling the individual from the social sphere, depriving him of his condition as a citizen, reducing him to the category of a mere member of the species.

25. Fina Birulés pointed out to me the relation between this statement and the one Peter Berger made in his article "El extraño caso de Giorgi Morandi" (*El País*, February 7, 1997): "Traces are not just what remains when something has disappeared, they can also be the marks of a project, something to be revealed."

CHAPTER 3

Nostalgia for the Horizon

1. *By way of introduction.* Will the future remember this generation as the one that ushered in a new time, that began a journey down a different road? Or will they look at it ironically as the one that dreamed the bittersweet dream of postmodernity, the one that repeated the gesture of the *tabula rasa* for the thousandth time in history? This is the question posed by John Donne in his *Divine Poems*: "What if this present were the world's last night?" These are not questions to be answered, but open ones to be followed up, like regulatory horizons, in this discourse — the only way we know to mark the confines of what we can think.

In times of beggary, we lack for nothing. We might say that this is the strange paradox of contemporary man. On the one hand, he dwells on his losses and defeats, his crises and failures to the point of morbidity; he faces posterity with his greatest gesture of pain. On the other, he gazes at the past with haughty indifference: he knows its confines and its nature. He thinks there is nothing to hope for from it since he discovered that it is a construction of his own. But the paradox hides an inner lack, which reveals itself on particular occasions. And so certain ways of dismissing an author (saying that "he belongs to a time that is no longer ours," for example) take for granted what authors should demonstrate — that is, that we know what is proper to our own time, what constitutes it.

Knowledge of a reality does not come from the mere fact of being in it, nor even from the fact of taking part of it. People still talk as if immediacy were a guarantee of truth, as if being close to something brings a direct understanding of it. When in fact that has always been the problem: to be capable of being surprised by something that has always been there. To turn the situation we have just mentioned around, that is why a certain way of praising an author — for example, arguing that time has proved him right, or that he saw what everyone accepts today — is tantamount to remaining in the exterior of his thought. It is to give him a eulogy that does not concern him. To take him as a pretext for our search for reinforcement.

2. *Where the problem is.* There is nothing new in what we are saying. As opposed to what people sometimes think, reflections on history point to the present (if possible, to put it in someone else's words, to the heart of the present). There is something of a methodological procedure, a testing ground for measuring our own self-awareness about the trip around the past, the recourse to events that have already happened. Perhaps the misunderstanding that the historian is exclusively concerned with the past and that the philosopher of history, who accompanies him on his journey, devotes himself to speculating on the meaning of that erasure is related to theoretical suppositions that no longer work. When men lived in the conviction of the continuation of the human race, when they looked at themselves in the example of earlier generations like someone looking in a mirror, the backward gaze blended curiosity about the past and interest in the present into a single gesture.

Today that has changed, as it seems, irreversibly. There is no way of ignoring the fact that contemporary man feels new, *another*. He lives in the conviction that he is settled on the far side of a break. His reality has nothing to do with the reality of those who went before him in the use of words and life. How much is true of such a conviction and how much is fiction? Elucidating that may be one of the most useful tasks the philosopher of history could apply himself to in these times. Before, that awareness of a break was almost exclusively associated with the (inevitable) dreams of an adolescent, that charming character who calls himself the inventor of everything he discovers. In our time that attitude has become widespread, largely as a result of the near hegemony of the mass media in the shaping of awareness.

We are familiar with the deep logic they respond to. Perhaps the best way of picturing what philosophers obscurely refer to with labels such as *fragment* or *loss of totality* is to show the operation of any of those media and most of all the attitude they end up creating in their consumers. Readers of newspapers or viewers of the television news sit down to them wanting to be surprised. "Let's see what's happened today," they say, with the secret expectation that the headlines will provide them with some forceful intensity, the more unexpected the better. And so when I was preparing this work the information highlighted everywhere was the tragedy of Zaire (which was spoken of in terms of "the greatest mass movement in history"), but I am sure that when it is read the issue will have fallen into total oblivion, though no doubt the problem that caused it will remain unsolved.

What is absolutely not the point in the media is to look for a guiding thread, to follow through an argument, to try to reconstruct a globality. We have to start from scratch every day, seems to be the slogan. As Borges said, books are made for memory and newspapers for oblivion. But let us not draw from that quotation the complacent, gratifying interpretation that we are in the right place. Let us, rather, think which of the two procedures most models the collective imaginary and draw the relevant conclusions. With their permanent invitation to the logic of starting from scratch, the mass media are shaping a particular way of thinking about the world, a certain attitude where the stress is placed on the idea of novelty. In the world of today any attitude presented as inaugural is welcome. Expressions like *let's start afresh, let's move on* or *a new transition* seem, almost from the moment they are uttered, to be loaded with positive connotations.

However, it might be more worthwhile for our purposes to emphasize what is excluded: memory. There is something anomalous, deeply unhealthy about a society that cannot bear to think of itself in terms of the past, that refuses to recognize itself in what it was, that theorizes discontinuity, break, to the point of delirium. But to show what we are referring to we need not scale the highest peaks of theory either. We can point out what we are referring to in our most immediate, most everyday reality. We live in a time when to remember what someone said just two or three years ago (and if it was in an election campaign, even less) is seen as in bad taste, something aesthetically ugly. A wretched theoretical recourse, in short.

Those who adopt that voluble attitude usually defend it in the same way: "don't we have the right to change?" To put it in those terms shifts the ground where the issue is to be tackled. To deny that supposed right would obviously be tantamount to adopting an indefensible inquisitorial attitude, to imprisoning individuals in their past commitments — denying them their freedom, in short. Perhaps the question should be answered with another question: "don't we have the right to ask about the reasons for the changes?" In case it is not clear, we are arguing against the systematic forgetting of the past.

We have introduced the adjective "systematic" quite deliberately. I am not referring to the Nietzschean forgetting — necessary to stay alive according to the idea of the *Untimely Meditations* — to which developed Western societies apply themselves with gusto for the sole purpose, it seems, of deactivating subjectivity. Without leaving the plane of the most everyday reality we should give another example, supremely representative of the modern world. The phenomenon of fashion most effectively illustrates the kind of person certain social structures are determined to produce: a weak, malleable, manipulable one.[1] Totally willing to uncritically accept what are usually called the changing *dictates* [*sic*] *of fashion*. Once again, what needs emphasizing is the readiness of the consumer (in this case of fashion), the fact that he adapts uncomplaining to something presented as supremely gratuitous, unjustifiable. For if there is anything that needs no alibis it is fashion, of which one of the main attractions is the daring with which it assumes its condition as whim, as an idea lacking the support of any arguable criterion.

True, there have been interpreters who have assessed this phenomenon in a quite different light. They have said that a different approach should be taken to fashion, insofar as its specificity consists of offering individuals a new chance to transform their appearance. That places the emphasis, so to speak, on the objectivity of the idea: fashion must be appreciated for what can be done with it. But our previous insistence on the attitude, on the willingness of subjects — whether with information or fashion — in some way foreshadowed the reply to this argument. The true issue is not the abstract possibilities fashion supplies the consumers with, but their real capacity to activate them.

This is not a merely rhetorical objection, much less marginal to what we are talking about. For if individuals have no independent criteria to determine themselves with — and, as we have just seen, it seems useless to ask that of fashion — all the supposed possibilities offered by it are no longer liberators. Technically today it is possible to change one's own body, transform it as one wishes, model it according to the preferred canon. And so the question is: is that leading to an explosion of differences or, on the contrary, are we witnessing the apotheosis of homogenization? There is only one answer that could be sustained, so much so that the nature of the process is the opposite of what its theoreticians claim: diversity is in a previous reality (the diversity of bodies or of appearances in general). The problem is to recognize that.

The argument may be satisfactory, but it is in no way conclusive. One question, the really important one, remains open: the reason for the social efficacy of these phenomena. So it is the answer to that question that should enable us to take up the thread of our discourse again. Fashion functions in this society because it feeds the fantasy that we can *be someone else at will*. Fashion turns that striking incapacity of contemporary man to recognize himself in his past into a habit, a custom, a regular social practice. The nervous laugh with which we reject our own image in that photograph of a few years ago would no doubt remind a psychoanalyst of the uneasy hilarity with which so many people react when subjects related to sexuality are broached. Fashion loans us the arguments for strangeness: "with those clothes," "with that hair" ... There is both unease and relief in a reaction of that kind: what we might have been worries us, but we are pleased to think we managed to escape from it.

We have to say this to prevent any misunderstanding: the least of it here is fashion as such. Our reaction to our own image is an expressive and faithful indicator of our reaction to our entire past, our reaction to ourselves. That is why there is no contradiction between what we have been arguing so far and the fact that in our society a certain way of relating to the past, what we might call the nostalgic variant, has become general. The reason why that specific incursion into what has happened has not been taken into account has to do precisely with the function it performs, the particular darkening effect it has on individuals.

Nostalgia, as expressed in any of the retro fashions that are periodically offered us from different spheres, is not a knowledge option. It does not set out to confront individuals with their truth or help them accede to their own identity. Quite the opposite, it seems to be surreptitiously aimed — rather like those disaster or terror movies — at a certain reconciliation with what exists. What is evoked by nostalgia is by definition something one cannot remain in, an imaginary object that only allows aesthetic contemplation. After that sweet gaze at what is irretrievably lost, it only remains to return to the warmth of reality, which, as we come in from the cold, looks more comfortable, more habitable, than when we went out there, into our own past. That one-line poem ("Old Friends Meet") by a Mexican poet is irritating in its perfection: "We are everything we fought against when we were twenty." The poet may have been seeking to irritate the reader. Perhaps the first thing we need to fight against today is that kind of perception, that unhealthy, resentful striving to present life as always on the verge of fulfillment.

3. *Where the solution is.* The worst is over. It is not too risky to argue that the most difficult moments for historical sensibility occurred in the 1980s. The crisis of Marxist thought (of which the fall of the Berlin Wall was the final episode, the moment that demonstrated Lukacs's accurate description of practice as the consummation of theory) that began in the mid-1970s had been undermining the central pretension of its speculative discourse.

The pursuit of scientific knowledge in history had become an aim as useless as it was undesirable: science was the expression of the ideal of domination on the plane of knowledge and history, once defined as a new continent, had sunk like a new Atlantis into the waters of the present. At that time, so we were told, we were living in post-history, the hoped-for event had been left behind. History was now no more than a still-fresh corpse with nails and hair still growing but which only a dupe or an ignoramus would take for a living body.

But there were also other perspectives in those years that, starting from apparently different presuppositions, fundamentally coincided in their diagnosis. In the end the thesis, so vilified at the time, of the end of history confined itself to trying to pose in philosophical terms what was a widespread state of opinion in the 1980s. The idea, in short, that the way of organizing public life represented by the developed Western democracies was an irreversible model and the idea of going beyond it was unthinkable. The only task remaining to the societies that had already reached that model was to apply themselves to perfecting its operative device (in the final battle between fragmentary social engineering and the revolutionary transformation of the totality, Popper won by a knockout). The only path open to the ones that had not was to close the distance that separated them from the others. The controversy it sparked was as noisy as it was timely and relentlessly showed up the suppositions of more than one person. Today we can say, somewhat simplistically — and somewhat provocatively — that that philosopher, stigmatized for collaborating with the US Department of State, had tried to theorize the common sense of a decade, the commonplaces that had been trotted out so often that they were beginning to be unviable. The reaction it provoked seems to demonstrate that there are few things men can bear less than having their own thinking shown up.

But all that is well known and not worth dwelling on too long. On the other hand, it is important to emphasize the drift events have followed since then, the new sensibilities they seem to point to and the paths that can be glimpsed through the undergrowth. The key appeared earlier when we pointed out that the purpose of certain social structures is to deactivate subjectivity. It will be useful to retrieve that idea for what remains, among other things because it will allow us to make it clear from the outset that a complaint about a particular situation is not lodged from equally impossible theoretical attitudes.

Some people might think, for example, that those earlier laments conceal something like a yearning for a utopia. The truth is that if there is something worth yearning for it is utopianism — that is, the capacity some people in the past gave a voice to for generating great collective projects with a universal calling — rather than utopia, which we can probably recognize today in its genuine state as a commitment to a perfect future on a horizon occupied by imperfect futures. Since we only mentioned it before, let us now quote the blunt statement, half hidden among the footnotes of *The Human Condition*, which Arendt let fall: "Utopia is the 'opium of the people' which Marx believed religion to be."

Likewise, it would be an even more serious error of perspective to interpret the defense of the territory of subjectivity in terms of a one-dimensional individualism. The criticism leveled at the systematic production of forgetting cannot be misinterpreted as a private reproach. We should not fall into the sin (of pride) of making our own sensibility a criterion. In the end, for the individual neither forgetting nor remembering is the object of a decision: there are resistant images that remain, like open wounds, at the heart of our present, while others return us when we least expect it to the melancholy sepia of our youthful memory. That is not what matters now. If we were to identify the territory of subjectivity with the confines of the individual we would be giving up the last hope of salvation.

Benjamin, himself the guardian angel of a large part of present-day historical sensibility, had already suggested the figure we can represent ourselves in. History is still the place to think from because everything is there. And not just because everything constructed is there but also for something far more important: because it is the only sphere where we can locate that secret order that constitutes us. To turn our backs on it is tantamount to giving up any expectation of meaning, to assuming the present as fate, as destiny. Our habit — if not our desire — of finding symmetrical figures can play a nasty trick on us on occasions like this. We do not always oppose a thought with another of an opposite nature, just as we do not always confront a particular promise with an opposite imaginary future. Those who are in favor of the closure of reality, those who theorize the exhaustion of the possible, no longer have any doctrine other than non-thought. The supreme argument of the defeat of any historical alternative to what there is now allows them to retrieve the discourse of the obsolescence of all discourse, so typical of conservative attitudes for some decades. And so they repeat for the thousandth time the attempt to liquidate the political space, to turn it into a mere administration of resources. Their language has ended up becoming familiar: we have to talk about goods instead of rights, debts instead of responsibilities, taxpayers instead of citizens . . . Nothing bothers them more than when some people affirm their condition as subjects, defend their will to intervene at the heart of what exists now from an explicitly assumed reflective identity.

If we unburden the term of its circumstantial connotations, we might call that intervention political action: participation in that common, open, public sphere of the *polis*. The only place indeed where what was once called a collective subject can occur. But it should be made clear that the political action we need now will have to combine fidelity to its own tradition with the imagination indispensable for meeting the new challenges. Let no one be under any illusions: memory is not made to turn us into pillars of salt, nor does the will to intervene in reality doom us to putting up with everything. Caution should not blur the ultimate aim of this role. If there is something to emphasize it is the need to recover the idea of the future or, to put it another way, the urgency of fighting that ferocity of the present that is so typical of our times. To be in favor of the possible — which is like a commitment to history going on because the game is not over yet — has become a question of survival.

Note

1. In his book *L' individualismo proprietario* (Turin: Bollati Boringhieri, 1987) Pietro Barcellona has provided interesting arguments about this. He has pointed out the extent to which the structuring, typical of modern society, of the formal abstraction of legal equality and the quantitative

abstraction of mercantile equivalence inevitably ends in the abdication of subjectivity and its dissolution in the empty mass individualism of consumption.

CHAPTER 4

An Opportunity for a Different Identity
(More on Tolerance)

1. *First words.* About the concept of tolerance we could say something similar to what Ricoeur says about action — that is, that in order to understand it properly we have to set it in a broader conceptual framework, which he proposed to call the *conceptual network of action.* Tolerance has a stronger tie with neighboring concepts than mere association or complement. That is why there is nothing random about the fact that merely to pronounce the word inevitably refers us to notions such as barbarism, multiculturalism, cosmopolitanism, racial mixing or difference (to name but a few: there are more, as we shall see). That reference should be understood not as a sign of the weakness of the category, but of the complexity of the situation it is applied to.

For only from such a perspective can we duly understand the reappearance of this issue at this particular moment. In other words, attacks on the idea of tolerance often use the argumentative strategy of detaching it from its material and intellectual context as a weakening premise that leaves the critic with the ground clear for his attack. That does not mean that a sure effect of placing it in a proper context is protecting the category from any questioning, simply to point out that setting it in its proper framework is a precondition of intelligibility.

2. *A trip round the city.* So, if we have to begin by making some reference to the material context, it is inevitable to allude — little more than that: other participants in this volume have touched on this — to those phenomena that are as characteristic of the present historical moment as the development of communications, the mass migrations and the rise of the immense cit-ies — the so-called megalopolises. Phenomena that are evidently profoundly interrelated but that, if only for the purposes of exposition, may need to

be tackled separately. That point should not be interpreted as a specialist's scruple. The fact is that things are not conceived identically in different spheres. If we look at the first two phenomena we see that the difference is so great that it may even seem contradictory. While the development of communications refers to what we might call the *friendly side* of globalization, the great migrations show us the harsher, surlier face of the new processes. As has been pointed out on more than one occasion, what in the field of information or capital is free circulation without borders of any kind is a restriction, an often insuperable obstacle, when it comes to people.

The specific nature of the third phenomenon has to do with its greater generalization. The big cities are what we might call the new reality, the privileged territory where the modalities of any conflict can be most effectively analyzed. Postindustrial society is almost totally urbanized. The world is the city or, to turn it around, the city is the *new nature*. The old nature is only our prehistory now, something we should conserve for reasons that lie somewhere between melancholy and survival, but which occupies quite another place in our imaginary representation of the world. It is no longer *the exterior* that surrounds humanized spaces (an exterior that still seems to be present in expressions like "a day out in the countryside"), but the opposite. And so we talk about *nature reserves* or propose laws that regulate *access to nature* (an expression that turns the classic image on its head: now it is nature that is surrounded — though it might be more accurate to say besieged — by the city). Today the city is, as traditional philosophical language would put it, *the given*: what we can count on, the reality to which there is no alternative starting point. By maintaining that we are taking a step beyond the simple statement that everything happens in the city, we are saying that the concept of society has been absorbed by the city, as proved by the fact that in our everyday language the word *society* on its own, as it appeared in the discourse of the 1960s to put a recent date on it, is tending to disappear — or at least to be burdened with ingenuously anachronistic connotations. Now everything is city. Which would confirm Marx's old intuition: just as the whole of history is contained in the city-country antithesis, the destiny of the modern city sums up the future of humanity completely. In Europe, in America and in Asia we can find a series of big cities that are both the places where economic wealth is concentrated and the centers of political activity and cultural production. Better to put it that way than to plunge into the thicket of a categorical distinction between recent hyperurban concentrations (like Mexico City or Singapore) and old European cities (like Paris, Berlin or Vienna). There is no doubt of the host of features that differentiate them,[1] but there are more things that unite them than separate them or, which comes to the same thing, there is no doubt that the former are the children of the latter — and in a way their destiny.

We should not lose sight of those last statements, because the characterization of the city in terms of a referent that substitutes for the old nature has the disadvantage of not sufficiently emphasizing the dimension that will be of most interest to us from now on. On the one hand, it is mistaken to think of the city in the same way as nature because, unlike it, the city is a product, a result of our activity. That statement is quite obvious, and yet it seems to have been forgotten in that consideration, so frequent in the language of the man in the street, of the city as a web of services and possibilities within his reach, which is there with the same mixture of need and availability as trees and birds are in nature. On the other hand, the absorption of the idea of society by that of city can give rise to its own errors, such as supposing that the problems linked to the absorbed concept have been overcome. But the point is not so much to stop thinking about the old problems of society and concern ourselves with the problems of the big cities as the latter have to be thought about in this new theoretical framework.

Which means reviewing the traditional ways of understanding social conflicts and the idea of the city together. Some may find this rather unattractive, insofar as they gather that the proposal is to visualize today's big cities as the new stage for a struggle that was never concluded. But anyone making that objection should begin by acknowledging that all too frequently in recent times the discourses of many theoreticians of the cities have moved toward a conciliatory, exaggeratedly bland language that excludes any antagonism, any rough edge, from the discourse.

Nevertheless, the city is not only that, precisely because, as we have just said, it is everything. The city is not the mechanical result of adding up festivals, infrastructures and services. It is the space of sociality, a sociality that today can only be heartbreaking, painful. How outdated in so little time has the expression *model of society* become, the channel for all differences before. But conflicts do not vanish just because we stop talking about them. It would not be good for that image of social reality that people from other spheres try to impose on us with the supreme argument of the defeat of any other historical possibility to penetrate the discourse of the city as well. That image structures the thousandth conservative attempt to do away with politics, to turn everything into a mere administration of resources. (On occasion I have taken the liberty of calling that attempt the fantasy of the accountant politician.)

The city is also difficulty in living, in being what one wants, in aspiring to what one believes one has a right to. The city also has a hard, rough, violent face that we cannot turn a blind eye to. The debate that has exploded in our faces is how much inequality we are prepared to put up with. It is no accident that we have ended up associating the image of the totally empty city with the day after destruction.

We are pointing all this out to prevent any possible misunderstanding. It would not make much sense to make do with a generic statement such as "the city is the people who live in it." Among other reasons because with that attitude — in short, a deliquescent variant of humanism, which might deserve the label of populist humanism — what would be surreptitiously creeping in is a similarly *well-meaning* consideration of the notion of tolerance, hinting without being explicit that the reason why it is so often invoked in debates today is because we need to promote more respectful attitudes to difference in an increasingly complex, multicultural world in order to bring about the necessary coexistence. That will not be the idea in what follows, nor does it give the impression that this journey will yield very much in the way of theory.

3. *Back already.* Even more, it may well be a treatment like the one mentioned (tolerance as a virtue, that is[2]) that goes a long way to explaining the reactions of rejection of this idea, reactions that have also proliferated in recent times. Almost all of them stress that the idea of tolerance does not think about, and therefore never questions, the specific reality in which the conflict between differences occurs. The observation that tolerance usually implies hierarchy is fair: there is someone who tolerates and someone who is tolerated. The relation is, therefore, not horizontal; it is not a relation between equals. If we think, for example, of cultural differences, we can easily see to what extent, both in the past and now, that supposed fusion or overlap that is usually called a racial mix has in fact amounted in a fairly short term to a deculturization.

This is not the moment, because we would undoubtedly end up straying into theoretical fields far removed from the one we want to visit, to examine how far this neglect of the global perspective is a symptom of our time. It could be alleged that the neglect cannot be exclusively imputed to the defenders of a certain idea of tolerance, but has become a typical feature of the current mentality in many modern societies. It is true that we can detect an identical neglect in many other discourses, even in some that expressly propose intervention in social reality. That is the reproach that has been leveled at the defenders of the "0.7%" campaign: not taking into account the political situation of the underdeveloped countries that are to receive the aid, thus triggering a whole series of perverse effects. But it is clear that the allegation does not vary the substance of the argument. That this neglect is widespread does not justify it in the least. In any case, the cry of the different person — I don't want to be tolerated — is still fair and quite right.

In the face of all this, the most useful — and clarifying — thing is to deal with the kind of economic, political, social and cultural relations that have been established in the new urban concentrations. For all there is still a spatial isolation of communities and we can still talk of an Arab quarter in Paris, a Puerto Rican district in New York or a Jamaican suburb in London the fact is that the model of *the city within a city* that might have been possible at some time in the past is becoming ever less feasible. If these new citizens still had the same kind of relations with their neighbors in other districts that they did in the past, for example the Chinese immigrants enclosed in their Chinatown in some US cities, most of the conflicts that arise now would never have happened.

At the same time, if we think of the complexity and variety of situations the real theoretical difficulty of the issue emerges more clearly — a difficulty that is often hidden when things are put in certain terms. In certain discourses, cosmopolitanism or racial mixing are loaded with positive connotations, just as the mere mention of expressions like ethnic purity or standardization conjure up undesirable realities. But to operate in this way, leaving the discourse to glide down the comfortable slope of marked words, may give rise to certain confusions, if not to flagrant contradictions.

Certain intransigent behaviors are not always assessed in the same way according to the cultural framework of those who perpetrate them. So they may be regarded as a legitimate defense of certain traditions in the face of the advance of the uniform developed Western model or, on the contrary, an unjustifiable display of hegemonic pretension when they are done in the name of some universal principle (for example, the defense of certain rights). Another frequent case is the defense by a developed society of the model of the integration of cultures (deploying the full panoply of the rhetoric of coexistence as required), which may be regarded as an unacceptable interference — a kind of cultural fifth column — when proposed by less developed societies. We should be warned — for the moment just in passing: later the theoretical elements that underpin the criticism will be presented — about the consequences of this contamination of the discourse by politics. For to allow a questionable idea to be criticized when those who propound it are in positions of power, but not when they are oppressed by the powerful, seems to lead us toward a *double epistemological morality* that is difficult to defend. But to try to deactivate the criticism of the oppressed by the powerful with the most properly theoretical argument — which we shall also refer to later — that the central epistemological categories of the latter are inexorably linked to particular points of view, leads to the symmetrical and inescapable conclusion that the criticism of the powerful by the oppressed is also valueless.

4. *What else we are talking about (for example, freedom and equality).* One way out of these difficulties may be to try to pin down the content of the concept of tolerance that may help to clarify matters in the context of the present discourse. Which is to say that we prefer to speak in terms of definition rather than proposal. From this perspective, the suggestion that arises now is to try to analyze the categories involved in the development of the concept as we have looked at it so far. With the previous terms, the reference to the material context needs to be completed by that other reference we began this work with, the intellectual context. By operating that way, we see that the concept of tolerance has strong theoretical links with other concepts.

So the earlier consideration about the element of hierarchy that, according to some, is inherent to the notion of tolerance implied — as could probably be deduced from the tone — a negative valuation of the phenomenon. That is precisely what moved us to describe as fair the protest inherent to *I don't want to be tolerated*[3]: a tolerance of that kind would not question the nature of the reality it is to be applied to. In short, a correct interpretation of the idea of tolerance involves properly establishing the theoretical links between that idea and, first and foremost, the idea of equality.

It has no doubt been the sum of the ambiguity of both terms that has given rise to a theoretical situation in which it is difficult to reach even a minimal agreement as to what the relevant questions are, the ones that should be used to start to think about the issue. A very simple example: it is not insignificant, as an even slightly careful look will see immediately, to propose "all men are equal" as an unquestionable basic affirmation or replace it with "they are equal to us." The specific ambiguity of the concept of equality is related here to the confusion between conceptual pairs. As we have known since Hegel,[4] the opposite pole of equality is not difference, but inequality. The pair of difference is identity.

But this point does not magically solve all problems. Equality has something to say about differences: it is no more nor less than the guarantor of their right to exist. However, acknowledgment of that right is not the last word of the argument, but the first. Why do we take it for granted that there is an argument? Because equality should not be confused with equivalence. True, there are authors in the past who proposed — or at least encouraged — that identification, but past errors, for all the authority those who made them may have had, should be regarded rather as an opportunity to learn than a design in which to persevere.

One of the most famous ways[5] of posing the issue within the specific sphere of cultural anthropology is represented by Claude Lévi-Strauss. His theses about the nonexistence of "savage thought," as opposed to a supposed "civilized thought," are complemented with the statement that the structure of our culture is as much of a myth as any other. From there it is easy to imagine what his attitude will be when invited to take part in the debate about the clash of cultures. Lévi-Strauss defends — in a deep sense: that of their respective structures — the difference of cultures. Insofar as that means rejecting the existence of a privileged, superior culture, from which it would be possible to criticize any other cultures, we can classify his attitude as *cultural relativism*.

However, it would be a mistake, only taking account of the author's professional dedication, to understand his defense of cultural relativism — or, to put it the other way around, his criticism of ethnocentricity — as merely technical, as if the argument were entirely based on epistemological reasons, when in fact suppositions of a philosophical character play a highly influential part in his conclusion. By way of illustration of what we mean we might mention his treatment of the idea of progress. Lévi-Strauss disagrees with the commonplace that it only makes sense to talk of progress in relation to our culture. It is true, he acknowledges, that it contains notable rhythms of transformation that have shown a substantial capacity for assimilating novelties of all kinds, but it does not follow from that that there is no progress in societies less accelerated than ours. There is, just as the history of Western civilization often seems more like a retrograde step toward disintegration and destruction than an advance. We might say that, consistent with what he has been saying throughout his work, what Lévi-Strauss is proposing is not to reject the concept of progress but to make it relative.

Naturally, this is not the moment to enter into an argument about the specific ideas of the author of *Tristes Tropiques*. Nor should we have any problem acknowledging the positive effects of his treatment of the issue. The best thing about his reflection is its invitation to linger in this territory of difficulties, to raise a legitimate doubt about whether everything is worth the same and, in any case, to make explicit the problem of how to go beyond a mere realization of difference. The negative part of his approach is probably the tendency to identify tolerance with equivalence.[6]

Searching for the links between the ideas of tolerance and equality naturally involves setting the former in the larger framework of the program of the Enlightenment or, which comes to the same thing, thinking about it in its relation to the discourse of democracy.[7] That does not mean that there are no variants of this idea to be found at earlier moments of history (for example, among the first Christians or certain currents of thought in Antiquity[8]), but rather that its definitive impulse and fullest materialization occur when the great principles of the modern democratic states are structured. We shall observe that by establishing this, far from devaluing any of the earlier formulations of the concept of tolerance, the idea is to analyze them in the light of the political destiny that awaited them. Perhaps one of the cases in which this ultimately political scope becomes most evident is that of Bartolomé de Las Casas, analyzed by Fernández Buey[9] from a point of view close to the one we are commenting on, though with identical arguments we could also mention the cases of Voltaire[10] or Montaigne.[11]

In all of them the attitude of respect for differences — or the reverse, the decided rejection of any form of fanaticism or obscurantism — is based on a conviction of the existence of a common stock of rationality in all men that must not be obscured — far less devalued — behind the diversity of more apparent customs ("reason reigns everywhere and [. . .] thought is just in any place where there are men," wrote La Bruyère). Anything of cultural relativism there might be here, therefore, is not exactly identified with the content with which we are accustomed to understanding that expression, still less insofar as that relativism tends to appear today as the only possible alternative, once we have established the impossibility of locating a really universal idea of reason (or are horrified by the excesses committed in its name).

As opposed to this skeptical-agnostic interpretation of relativism, those authors base tolerance on the principle of universal equality, attribute it a content, to put it another way. Hence theirs is not an impotent relativism but a hopeful one. Which does not throw in the towel of knowledge at the first signs of change: does not give up posing the problems involved in making the affirmation of difference simultaneous with the postulation of a universal rationality. The least of it now is the particular form in which those thinkers try to find a way out of these difficulties (for example, by distinguishing between customs and civilization proper).[12] What really matters is their shared determination to struggle to free men from superstition, the prejudices of dogmatism and the cruel violence of fanatics. We should recall all that, not only to place their ideas in their due context but also for something far more important: to place ours in an appropriate one. It would not do for us, exclusively concerned with one of the manifestations of the problem (for example, the excesses of ethnocentrism), to fail to see that what many manifestations of intolerance show is a rejection of the principle of equality.[13]

If we were to make do with that, we could no doubt reproach the previous order of considerations with its exaggeratedly programmatic character, the fact that things could have been conceived as if it was a matter of deciding between *tolerance yes* and *tolerance no*, when the issue has always been to elucidate which notion of tolerance is acceptable and what to do to make it an instrumental notion (and not a regulatory virtue for approaching some ideal coexistence). When we began to talk about equality, we remarked on the difficulty of having to choose between statements of the "all men are equal" or "they are equal to us" kind (although we would have similar difficulty with slogans like "do not wish for others what you do not wish for yourself" or that other one, used some time ago in Spain for an institutional campaign in favor of tolerance, "do you really think you are better than them?"). And so now we can see better that what is at stake in such choices is the direction the concept of tolerance should be developed in, whether toward universality or toward ethnocentrism. But to talk in terms of development (or process) is to put forward the following argument, to begin to say that an option of this nature is not resolved by dwelling on the (impossible) comparison between the legitimacy of universalist and ethnocentrist reasoning, but by incorporating into the argument the other basic concept of the program of the Enlightenment: freedom.

And we need to enrich the debate with another concept because, owing to the very nature of the idea, the reference to equality alone may not be enough. As Todorov rightly says,[14] tolerance based on equality cannot be subject to any limits, in the same way that we say that any unequal discrimination is to be condemned. The issue we need to tackle is whether a position like this implies moving toward an ethical relativism, in which anyone who appealed to tolerance would be giving up any value judgment about a culture other than his own on principle. But, depending on the situation, there should be no problem about acknowledging that a relativism of that kind can even be healthy. If, for example, we think of the case of foreigners, there is no doubt that introducing a dose of radical skepticism about the value of our own identity produces positive practical effects. But that situation by no means exhausts the casuistry. Then there are all those cases where the problems arise among equals. That is when we see that appeals such as for absolute equality before the law are not enough. Tolerance also needs freedom. Indeed, we have to acknowledge that human beings are equal but remain different. The question is, what happens when that difference generates a conflict?[15] For that is when the argument about the value of apparently boundless beliefs *comes down to earth* and obliges us to take decisions on a much more immediate ground. That is when we have to measure ourselves against those categorical convictions of Montesquieu that tyranny is an absolute evil anywhere and moderation an absolute good, and see what can be done with them (if we can do anything).

We are therefore not arguing that we must begin by acknowledging differences[16] — which is to say, by accepting the radical equality of all individuals.

But for that acknowledgment, that acceptance, not to remain an abstract proclamation, completely lacking in content, we have to decide the characteristics of that equality — that is, the list of rights and duties that constitute the individual as citizen.[17] To operate like that is to distance oneself from the concept that, basing itself on a certain way of understanding the public/private distinction, likes to present tolerance as a right of the individual conscience in the face of the interference of society (a concept in which the determination to introduce legal rules about certain customs in force in the home, for example, would clearly exemplify the state's incontinent urge to control every sphere of human life).

Of course, in itself the distinction between public and private is far from unambiguous, but this is not the time to enter into that debate. It would take us back (at least) to the Spinoza of the *Tractatus Theologico-Politicus*, the Locke of *A Letter Concerning Toleration*, their different ways of posing the relation between those two spheres and measuring the distance that separates those ways from ours. What needs to be stressed for the purposes of this work is that, even supposing we accept that freedom should rule in the private domain, in order to achieve that goal freedom has to be controlled in the public sphere. There are reminders that may be uncomfortable, but are unavoidable; if everyone did what they wanted, the limit of freedom would be strength, and the weakest would have no freedom at all (hence the slogan of feminist discourse: "the personal is political").

Nevertheless, even that concession to the relative autonomy of the private has to be administered with caution. Under certain descriptions we cannot continue to defend the principle of a freedom without restrictions in the private sphere. In the context of Spinoza's *Tractatus Theologico-Politicus*, which deals with the problems that spring from religious intolerance, it is easy to align oneself with the criterion that anyone should have absolute freedom to give an opinion and a judgment, and therefore, "speak also, provided he goes no further than the simple word, the simple teaching." But there are words that today are not just *simple words*. The twentieth century saw the spectacular development of technical communication instruments that have been rightly described as a means of shaping awareness. If after Austin it was impossible to ignore the fact that things can be done with words, after Adorno and the authors who have written in his wake we cannot be unaware that behaviors can be shaped with messages.

In other words, we should mistrust theoretical positions that maintain as a sacrosanct principle the existence of spheres that the public domain must not touch under any circumstances. If we usually accept as a theoretical conquest of contemporaneity that no value means anything in absolute or exclusive terms, it is hard to see why the private sphere should be declared outside the very possibility of control (which obviously does not mean effective control), as if the mere fact of being so constituted an absolute value (suspiciously, always without being determined).

The earlier idea of interpreting tolerance in political terms is thus being filled with content. If it is not determined in that direction, the defense of tolerance without restrictions may end up accepting the right to intolerance, and that, as Voltaire said, "is absurd and barbarous" (knowing that there is no greater barbarity than treating other people as barbarians). Unlimited tolerance, turning to an equally unrestricted idea of freedom, also ends up favoring the strong to the detriment of the weak. The resulting operation is — if I am permitted a moment of historicist weakness — a backward step, a pharisaic return to a supposedly Rousseauian prepolitical community. The operation recalls the cynical defense, which usually occurs in certain social and political contexts, of the category of *negotiation*, presented as the real possibility on a human scale of resolving conflicts, in the face of the colossal and alienated structure of the state and its legal procedures. Since we are recalling things, we should also recall that negotiation is only a value (a quite different matter is that it may be a way out) when we are dealing with a conflict of rights. Otherwise that is tantamount to submission to the dictates of *faits accomplis* (carried out by those who are in a position to do so), in the face of which negotiation is no more than a damage limitation exercise.

And so there is no contradiction in postulating the existence of intolerable acts. They would be the ones that endanger the very exercise of tolerance. And that exercise is jeopardized when the two basic values tolerance sets out to safeguard, those of equality and freedom, are attacked. That also happens on a collective scale when the democratic principle is attacked, what Locke called the social contract (that is, life in common in which independence is sacrificed to achieve protection), and when individuals suffer some kind of discrimination, by way of a wide range of intermediate situations. Which means that the fight for tolerance can take many shapes according to the particular circumstance, the particular flank the attack is coming from. There will be circumstances in which tolerance will be defended by rejecting any kind of discrimination — that is, by a demand for the unrestricted right to equality, and circumstances in which the tolerant will have to fly the flag of individual freedoms.[18]

This is not to cling to the evanescent argumentative resource *it depends*, but to try to take these premises to their logical conclusion. Once the problem is sketched this way, it is not surprising to realize that some have called it paradoxical, in the sense that since almost everyone agrees that we must practice tolerance because it is the only guarantee that freedom (which is one of our ideals) will be maintained, and knowing that in order to exist freedom must be limited, the outline of that limit will never be clearly drawn. And so now we can understand better that in fact what some people have called *liberal tolerance* (using "liberal" in the US sense) is based on that very apparent paradox.

Thomas Nagel[19] has discussed the statement made by Rawls in his famous work "Justice as Fairness,"[20] according to which if liberalism had to depend on a compromise with comprehensive moral ideas of autonomy and individuality, it would then be "another sectarian doctrine." Which is the same as saying, Nagel thinks, that liberal tolerance is not compatible with any other set of particular values and beliefs. Tolerance does not go beyond affirming itself (since it could not be any other way), which means simply demanding the conditions of possibility for its own existence. That is why a moment ago we talked of "safeguarding values" as a way of trying to show the relative exteriority with regard to any particular axiological program.

Which, of course, does not mean that the defender of tolerance lacks defined opinions about the problems that are valued irreconcilably by opposing points of view, or abstains from formulating value judgments about them. Whoever does that is not tolerant, simply perplexed and awaiting a destiny (i.e. awaiting the right convictions). What defines a tolerant person is not his lack of valuations of certain issues, but his attitude to other people's, especially when he is convinced that they are mistaken or false.[21]

But note a vital nuance: precisely because tolerance is not identified with a particular scale of values, it is not legitimate to present it as a virtue the ultimate justification of which lies in certain attitudes or feelings, such as altruistic ones. We shall not get very far by trying to base a defense of tolerance on altruism.[22] Besides, in case what we have said so far were not much, simple altruism does not offer a common position from which we can all come to the same conclusions. In fact, contractualism emerges to a large extent as a response to the evidence that altruism generates as many conflicts as there are concepts of good. That is one of the soundest arguments in favor of tolerance: because the best — the optimal — solution is not possible, we have to follow the model of choosing the best solution from the ones remaining.

This other way of arguing allows us to put that political dimension of tolerance we were talking about at the beginning in another light. Tolerance is, to use Iring Fetscher's expression, *a little virtue*. Little not because it is insignificant, but "because it depends on other institutional virtues and conditions without which it would lose its value." So nor is it any panacea, but that does not mean that we should jump to the basically mistaken conclusion that the discourse about it takes place on an exclusively superstructural plane, alien to men's most immediate and pressing problems. Tolerance — at this stage we may allow ourselves a certain solemnity — is as serious a matter as democracy itself. And one of the mistakes most often repeated in the past by supposedly progressive discourses may well have been their incapacity to recognize the transforming virtualities of reality offered by that way of organizing the public sphere.

5. *Lastly: tolerance, knowledge, identity.* However, now that we have dealt with those points, we would have no trouble acknowledging the element of truth in that observation. It is true that the debate on tolerance affects an aspect that elsewhere has been called the superstructure, or what some have preferred to call the collective imaginary. Our reservation is not to do with that, but with its disdainful valuation. For what is often at stake in the fight for tolerance is something of vital importance for both people and groups — that is, their own identity or, which comes to the same thing, the way we represent ourselves, the image of ourselves we are prepared to admit in the deforming mirror of those who are different.

As it has been argued, tolerance need not mean either making one's own ideas, habits and beliefs relative — as it is so often reproached with doing — nor an offhand paternalism toward other people's ideas, habits and beliefs. Nor is it relevant to argue about whether it is true that in practice, as Michael Walzer has said, "People kill one another for years and years, and then, mercifully, exhaustion sets in, and we call this toleration."[23] That undoubtedly happens (just as one can reach a defense of egalitarianism through compassion[24]), but that outcome would only be relevant if it expressed something like a destiny of the concept, not if it describes the debilitation of its users.

The tolerance that is worthwhile thinking about is, if you will permit me the expression, *affirmative tolerance*, the kind based on certain convictions. On the one hand, it is based on the sincere conviction — which we have commented on in part — that there are reasons for others to accept certain principles of tolerance, and that such acceptance does not require them to abandon their religious or moral positions, precisely because those principles neither deny nor exclude any set of particular values and beliefs. On the other hand, it is based on a conviction of a different kind — which is now beginning to come in — relating to one's own identity. If recognition of the other is a source of tolerance, that recognition calls for each person to know who he is.[25] Or, the other way round and on a larger scale, it is the lack of an identity of one's own that leads one to despise other nations, as Fetscher thinks.

Is what we are saying tantamount to arguing that someone who does not respect himself cannot respect others? At first glance it might be thought that proposing an equivalence of this kind means going beyond what the arguments put forward authorize. However, if we set it properly among the earlier ideas, we shall see that the equivalence is justified. In fact, the thesis that there is no knowledge of the other as other without self-knowledge returns us to the context of some of the initial statements about the *foundational spirit* of tolerance, places us once again in the thesis of the necessary link between this category and enlightened discourse. A link that can be examined from another angle.

For it would be mistaken to bring in the idea that tolerance is the necessary product, the obligatory result of the exercise of the greatest principles of the Enlightenment. The sleep of reason engenders monsters, how can we forget, but perhaps not its wakefulness. The difficulty of tolerance, what makes it a useless category in the opinion of many, is the very theoretical fact that it does not draw an unambiguous demarcation line; on the contrary, it can be attacked on more than one front. From as many fronts as the modern project is attacked, in short. And, a necessary clarification, that attack is carried out not only by those who expressly oppose its purposes with a scant variety of instruments (that curious *philosophical pincer* formed by post-Enlightenment hypercritics and theologizing precritics[26]) but also — and perhaps we should emphasize this now — those who distort their deepest purpose while claiming to abide strictly by it.

Such is the case of all those uses of modern Western rationality that, clinging to their legitimate pretension to universality, end up swallowing up differences, crushing them beneath their imposing uniformity machine. The adjective *legitimate* has been introduced here deliberately. There is nothing reprehensible about an aspiration to truth,[27] provided it is not at the expense of the pretensions of others. It is not that supposedly all-inclusive gesture that defines someone as intolerant (if that were so, if that were enough to discredit them, we would have to wonder: and who is more intolerant, assuming that there are degrees of intolerance, the one who affirms the truth of a universal culture or the one who affirms the truth of his particular culture? But can one believe in a culture, can one live in a fabric of convictions without believing in their truth?[28]), but the way that aspiration develops, in what way it approaches that horizon.

As in so many other spheres, in this one too it is best to think again about the program of the Enlightenment, not so much for what of it remains unfulfilled but, far more important, for the aspects in which it may have been directly betrayed. Far from leading to any kind of voracious intolerant rationalism, the will to knowledge, so characteristic of the modern European spirit, is a source of tolerance. It is from the urge to know the other that the virtue of tolerance has sprung. Note the positive — even *passionately positive* — link being proposed, quite different from that disdainful indifference with which some people identify tolerance. This other tolerance does not need to appeal, as an exterior regulatory element or an alternative, to the idea of respect, because it already has it incorporated, because it is a condition of the possibility of its very existence. In the face of scientistic pride or evangelizing fanaticism, united in their endeavor to turn the other into their own,[29] the enlightened tolerator treats the other specifically (and not at all paradoxically[30]): he regards him as an equal while recognizing him as different.

Here, in short, is the perspective — that of knowledge, as opposed to the different modalities of ignorance — we should adopt. And we should do so because the arguments often take a tone or a form that can undoubtedly lead to some confusion. Such is the case of so many victimist statements like "if you haven't lived this situation on the inside you can't really understand what is happening here." What they hide behind the appearance of a defense of the specific character of a certain reality, and thus the need for peculiar instruments (which usually ends up meaning empathetic instruments) to apprehend it, is a renunciation of knowledge. Merton pointed out many years ago that ideas of that kind end up in an explosion, a pulverization of the points of view behind which, at most, everyone knows about that particular, untransferable reality that is himself.[31]

That is also the grain of truth of the old reticence certain currents of thought, once bent on joining revolutionary progress and rationalism, displayed toward some classic forms of historicism, specifically all those that had at some time proposed as a model of historical knowledge the kind that managed to place the historian *in the place of* the protagonist of the past action in question (taking for granted that that was the place of *true knowledge*). To take one more step in Collingwood's criticism of this cliché, putting oneself in the other's place, respecting his difference, accepting his autonomy, is not the same as giving in to that other, assuming that, just because he is (himself), he understands his own reasoning, still less that he is right.[32] In this sense, "put yourself in my place" is perfectly symmetrical with "you will never understand me." And like it, it is a retrograde step in the development of self-knowledge.

It is not a matter of philosophical demagogy (or any other kind), but pretensions of the kind we are criticizing recall the argument that everyone must have heard on some occasion, the hoary old cliché "what would you do if you were the father, the husband, or the son, of someone who has been subjected to the most horrible atrocities? If you could get your hands on the person who did it you would . . . [and here there is usually some hair-raising suggestion] too" Perhaps the question should be different: would we like this to be the way society resolves conflicts of this kind? Would we think it right for society to leave the supposed perpetrators of certain crimes in the hands of the closest relatives of the victims and let them decide whatever punishment they consider appropriate? Or is the point of view of the person directly harmed the one we think the judge should adopt?

We should point out the twofold sleight of hand this way of arguing resorts to. Together with the fallacy we have indicated (of a fundamentally practical order) there is another difficulty, also important, that by appealing (emotionally) to an apparently unambiguous reality, the ideas we have mentioned shift the center of attention toward its protagonists and shift it surreptitiously without making the theoretical operation they are performing explicit. We know (at least since Anscombe) that there are a host of possible descriptions of a single action. If that is the case, the selection of the morally operative one must be crucial. It is obvious, to use the example given by Nagel,[33] that if someone believes that by restricting freedom of worship he is saving innocents from the risk of eternal damnation to which they are exposing themselves by deviating from the true faith, then *under that description* he might want others to do the same for him, since in the light of the fact that his is the true faith, his way to salvation might be barred.

We should be warned about an unrestricted use of this cliché, especially in view of the not very analytical causes at the service of which it is usually placed. Aside from the fact that Anscombe has referred at some point in his work to the existence of a *privileged* or *priority* description, which would affect the widespread interpretation that the multiple descriptions of an action are all on an equal footing, the truth is that the very idea of that plurality has been posed in such a way that it has led to major errors. Specifically, supposing that what we might call the web of the different descriptions might find its perfect correlate in extralinguistic spheres.[34]

It is true, for example, that any particular view of events can always be counterbalanced, in a court of law, by another of a completely different nature. But in any case such variety must be set in a channel preestablished by existing laws. And so we will have to decide first of all if we are pondering a crime or a misdemeanor, manslaughter or murder, culpable negligence or involuntary omission . . . and the diversity of versions seems to become less important in relation to these prior categories, so much so that one might even suspect that in fact each of the descriptions is the result of other less visible, but more fundamental — in the sense of constitutive — structures than linguistic ones. (Consequently, in order to be advanced the argument of the exchange of roles, which is feeble in itself, would require the prior condition of an unambiguously shared description of the same action.)

In view of all that, it is pointless to repeat that the doubt, reservation or suspicion (as the case may be) about what the other thinks he knows about himself can under no circumstances be understood, *a contrario*, as a declaration of paternalism. Evidently, reservations about the theoretical competence of the other do not in themselves guarantee one's own. But not having any complete guarantee is only a dissuasive argument about knowledge for those who still harbor hopes of absolute certainties or beliefs without fissures. Probably for those who hold such disproportionate expectations an encounter with the real limitations of our ways of apprehending reality, with the true scale of human knowledge, would arouse a feeling of disappointment.

In the face of that, the attitude of the thinker inspired by the principles of the Enlightenment is neither that of the metaphysical realist (things are *what they are* and the task of knowledge is to take note of that reality) nor the subjectivist skeptic (who turns the point of view of the protagonist of the action into the drain down which all discourse is lost, and his word into the last word).[35] He does not accept, either, *they don't understand us* or *you are wrong*, because what interests him is the construction of a universal place where, beyond any differences, we can all try to understand one another.[36]

Categories that are certainly not *precision* categories are being used. We are talking in terms of task and horizon, but that tentative language[37] should not be tantamount to blurring outlines and objectives more than strictly necessary. Each position has its own specific problems, and stating them will be the best proof that the task has contents and the horizon distance. To use expressions like "we need to tend toward . . ." in no way presupposes that what we find in the end will inevitably be some variant of universal reconciliation (a *fusion of horizons* or the like). Nor does it exclude it. More than that, it may even dare to proclaim it desirable, provided it is not taken as a mere voluntarist aspiration, with no content related to what has gone before. For the nexus may be of the opposite kind. If someone were to insist on defining the position maintained here as realistic, we would have to add that the realism proposed is aware of the commitments it may undertake. That is why it does not commit itself to the affirmation that there must be a single vocabulary in which objective truths would have to be expressed, only the weaker affirmation that once a vocabulary has been specified, the question of knowing whether the affirmations expressed in it are true or false has an objective answer.

The road to knowledge is undoubtedly paved with difficulties. The relation between people who are different often gives rise to communicative short circuits. To quote a famous case, in *On Certainty*[38] Wittgenstein gives the example of the argument between people who consult the physicist and those who consult the oracle and is not very optimistic about the possibilities of resolving the discrepancy. He claims (and the emphasis is in the text) that in that argument language games are *combating* one another. That statement and what follows ("where two principles really do meet which cannot be reconciled with one another, then each man declares the other a fool and heretic") have led some interpreters[39] to align Wittgenstein among the supporters — albeit in the subgroup of the resigned — of relativism.

Nevertheless, the nuances introduced later by Wittgenstein in the same text seem to support a more pondered interpretation of his points of view — an interpretation we would like to consider close to what we have been defending so far. Referring to what happens when missionaries convert natives, the author of the *Tractatus* proposes to draw a theoretical line showing the confines of the sphere of reasons beyond which there would only be persuasion. Put that way, the debate can probably be substantiated in whether those confines are to be understood as absolute and uncrossable or whether they must be visualized with the same image he used at other moments when trying to define the nature of language — that is, the image of limits man rages against in order to widen them, to push them back, to make room in the interior of what can be expressed linguistically for an ever greater volume of experience. The consistent relativist is obliged to opt decidedly for the first interpretation with no flagging and no concessions. To admit the tiniest variant of the ideas of tendency or process would be the beginning of the end for him. Through that crack the seed of dissolution would eventually slip inside his position. For at the moment when the idea that all the difficulties of communication between cultures or language games allow themselves to be read in some key is introduced, the intransigent initial solipsism (even if it is a solipsism with a *we* instead of an *I*) shows its deep inconsistency. To be radical, lack of communication must be inconceivable. Any statement with pretensions to truth must know that the truth is always internal to the given framework in which it takes place (for example, the corresponding language game).[40] But, taken to the limit, that attitude ends in the incoherent thesis that language as such is internal to one of its games.

Since there is no intention of caricaturing the positions of the litigants, it must be said that our imaginary relativist still has a bullet or two in the chamber of his argument. He can point out, for example, that that universal place in which his interlocutor claims to install himself — the place of *language in itself,* aside from any particular language game — is a nonexistent one.

The analogy Ricoeur has occasionally suggested with the dialogue among religions[41] might even come to his assistance, that the expectation of reaching a point of agreement between beliefs always resides in a determined specific faith: unbelievers never join in that kind of conversation.[42]

However, accepting that with a particular kind of entity, such as language in itself, there are no deals to be made — at least of the same kind we make with any of its games — does not condemn us to skepticism in theory and silence in practice. In the end, what is that thing we call metalanguage but the set of tools with which we try to grasp such a delicate, elusive object? What does our discreet enlightened man expect other than glimpsing a tiny silhouette on the horizon, an outline (however misty it may be) that tells him where he is and that he is steering the right course?

This last figure may give the relativist his next argument. The relations among those heterogeneous theoretical spheres (call them cultures, language games or whatever you will) are certainly dynamic and conflictive: who would dare deny the different interactions, ever more frequent in an increasingly globalized world? But the mistake, or the abuse of language — our imaginary character would be writhing around — is to attempt to give it any direction (so as to call it process or tendency). There is movement, true, but it is blind. There is no sign, no sense of direction, only an uncontrollable drift, a random shipwreck in the dark waters of the present.

Let us pursue the image a moment longer: with it there would have been no history of navigation. The relativist thesis can only be: we are as lost as we always were. Men's permanent desire to accomplish certain goals is the tale of an unfulfilled, tenaciously frustrated longing. The supposed history of knowledge is entirely resolved in dumb stupor. How could it be otherwise bearing in mind that, far from housing a metaphysics and an epistemology of serious truth and evidence, what has been called the "rhetoric of objectivity," in which the development of knowledge thought it had found its legitimacy, is in fact a mere game played by power, if not a way of silencing alternative ways of knowing. To prolong an argument about this issue ultimately makes no sense: concerning expressions of power (and nothing escapes this condition), it is not intellectual attitudes that should be proposed but political ones. What matters is not to refute but to defeat.

In the previous paragraph the term *history* appeared twice quite deliberately. The rejection of it is the perfect correlate of the denial of any possible communication among discourses. While the enlightened man we are thinking of here, we need hardly repeat, does not write off that communication, he trusts in being able to reach it and strives to provide the means that bring him close to it. But he does not discard the error or exclude the danger of taking the wrong road: that is the price he knows he has to pay for the affirmation of freedom, also in the field of knowledge.[43] Which is why there is no justification for mechanically attributing optimism to the defender of this position. According to Sartre's famous paradoxical phrase, we can be (at most) condemned to be free, but in no case can we be *condemned to improve*, because that would mean we do not have even the minimal freedom to get worse (which would be as absurd as denying the evidence of that possibility of destroying ourselves that is in our hands today). It is clear that there would be very little rationality and far less materialism about such a conviction. It would rather recall the providentialist "God writes straight with crooked lines" or the liberal "private vices, public virtues," with such a clear resonance that it would lead us to suspect that the two convictions might be two sides of the same coin. The suspicion urges us to be prudent: the only thing we can affirm — because it can be proved — is the will that seems to be behind the Enlightenment project and the resources it is equipped with.

That may be no small thing. Or perhaps a lot more than it seems. For once again the mere possibility is enough. The game stays open: we can even ask ourselves the most uncomfortable questions. The will behind the Enlightenment project matters if it manages to transcend awareness, if it manages to imbue our vision of reality, if, to put it in Ortegan style, it is transformed into *belief*. In its apparent insignificance, the spontaneous comment of so many people about the horrors the media regale us with every day, that simple "it seems incredible that something like that can happen today," is revealing. We should wonder, quite legitimately, whether that reaction was always the same throughout history. There are reasons for thinking that it was not, that for centuries men lived the web of pain and suffering they found themselves in — and that they produced — as something *given* and not something *done*. Not subject, therefore, to any imperative or responsibility.

If that transformation is true, we should wonder about the theoretical validity of regarding it as an indicator of some kind of *moral progress* the nature of which we would have to specify but if we needed a precedent we would find it in the Kant of *What is Enlightenment?* Of course, it would not be an absolute or unique indicator. We should hasten to point that out, because in certain philosophical circles expressions like the one just emphasized usually provoke an irritated reaction (what is suspicious about harboring some kind of hope?) and an immediate reading-over of the list of the horrors of the century. But it has not been precisely the enlightened perspective we have been trying to reconstruct that has called them in question or forgotten them. Incidentally, it is easier to find among the ranks of the relativists defenders of theses like "Auschwitz never happened" — or what might be its most perverse shift, the thesis that the real problem opened up by Auschwitz is not what happened but *how to recount it.*

Whoever gives any value to the repulsion men show toward violence, blunders or any form of barbarity does not do so from a pharisaic ignorance of the enormous (one might sometimes say inexhaustible) capacity for generating evil humanity has demonstrated since Antiquity. That last point may be unnecessary, but insofar as there is a misunderstanding behind it we should say something. It is difficult off the top of one's head to imagine anyone who might question that capacity. Like its opposite, the capacity to do good, it is in the usual sense a question of a practical order, fundamentally related to the development of scientific and technical knowledge. It is clear that, to take one milestone, since man discovered a way of killing at a distance, he has not ceased to perfect his skill at causing damage. But that skill still has no moral classification (the defenders of the military draw on that when talking about their deadly instruments as deterrents of those who threaten peace). For that technological development to be interpreted as a moral regression we would have to prove the indiscriminate rise of cruelty or at least (if we interpret the regression not as growing immorality but as the empire of amorality) the unstoppable spread of banality. And the other way round, of course. There is no moral progress in the discovery of certain medicines, however curative their effects may be, but there may be in the will that moved the search for them or the determination to apply the discovery to the benefit of the whole of humanity or, better still, of those who most need it.

To return to the original argument: if we can regard that "it seems incredible that . . ." as significant, if it gives us something to think about, it is because it is formulated from a clear awareness of the terrible power we possess, an awareness that in turn would be expressing in the chiaroscuro of the statement a desire that what are taken to be advances of humanity should not be lost. But, it should be emphasized, what good we have been capable of doing is not destiny, fate or inexorable design. We have produced it and for that very reason it is we who most threaten it.

Having said that, I could also qualify that brief allusion to optimism. There is only one reason to be optimistic and that is the trust that we are capable of simultaneously and systematically exercising the faculty that is most our own. But let there be no misunderstandings: to bring in, if only for a moment, terms like optimism or trust is not to take refuge in the indeterminacy of the ambiguous formula, but to expressly acknowledge the shortage of guarantees for our aspirations. Perhaps, just as some social scientists talk about the self-fulfilling prophecy, we should talk about the *self-defended prediction*, and assume that the successes unanimously regarded as positive conquests for the integral development of the human race should be real points of no return on our journey to the future.

Indeed, we may find some reference in the past that might be useful to exemplify what we mean, or perhaps as a model for what we should do. We could remind anyone who objected to our earlier idea that there is no human way of deciding those universally agreed successes that many of the demands we now regard as *prepolitical*[44] — that is, which we have agreed to definitively exclude from the particular political argument — were achieved at the time as a result of bitter and almost always painful struggles. From here we might now retrieve Marx's intuition of using the word "prehistory" for everything that would be left behind by humanity if it were capable of seizing the reins of its own destiny. History, then, far from having ended, would be actually beginning, i.e. men could cease to travel through the past like someone strolling through a gallery of mirrors or reviewing the catalog of his failures (according to whether one belongs to the satisfied or the unsatisfied faction of the troop) and go on to understand it happily as a journey toward a contingency[45] so full and so fully assumed that it would not even need the help of science ("if the essence and appearance of things directly coincided, all science would be superfluous" is the other dictum of Marx we should recover now).

Meanwhile, our situation is that of someone who is submerged in a prehistory (and a prepolitics) but does not know that it is one. But he knows something, and what he knows is important: if there came a day when some ideal (such as rationality in coexistence among men) prevailed, the triumph would be that of a *particular* model that can be given a time and a date (it emerged in Europe, at a moment of its history, etc). We cannot think otherwise once we give up any transcendent, metaphysical conception of human and worldly matters. Pointing out that origin like someone reporting a limitation can only be done from a position that would not have sufficiently internalized the immanence that philosophy itself (as opposed to theology, to be more explicit) incorporates as a foundational gesture. Should this be understood in the sense that there is no hope of universality? No, rather that the universality we can hope for will be of another kind. If that ideal were to prevail one day, it would become universal in its own way: from the fact that we would have been capable of agreeing about what *deserves to be shared* by all humanity. It would not be a (impossible) universality of origin but of destiny.

Let us end now, returning to the concept that triggered this whole reflection. It has been said that the most typical feature of European culture has been curiosity about the other, a curiosity that has led us, like Amerigo Vespucci, "to travel the world to see its wonders." This reminder of our spiritual origins may be particularly useful at the moment. There is a sense, bounded by the new conditions of possibility mentioned at the beginning of this work, in which it could be said that we are doomed to measure ourselves against our foundational situation.

Our fortune, not always a comfortable one, has been that history itself has taken charge of purging the mistakes made. We must know who we are in order to accept the other, true, but there is an old wisdom about ourselves that seems to have expired permanently.

I would not dare to say that our defeats have made us strong, but they may have returned us to our true scale, to our own condition. From the urge to know the other, the virtue of tolerance has sprung. Or, in any case, that is the only tolerance that interests us. The only adventure that matters is the one that resolves itself in knowledge, not the one that aims to culminate in a conquest. The conqueror, like the evangelist, has an excessive, intolerably strong identity, which can no longer be the case. In the face of that, to talk of a *weak* identity may lead to some unnecessary misunderstanding: the very idea of weakness was ruined some time ago through circumstances everyone knows about. There is weakness, but of another kind. Not so much the weakness of a mimic, but the weakness of a new dawn: the weakness of what could begin to take shape again.

The community we all carry inside ourselves has become the trigger for a conflict at a time when it has ceased to be a more or less homogeneous community (not even in struggle or in discord) and become confused, shapeless, perhaps in decomposition. The agreed collective stories have disappeared from our world, which has meant that the mechanisms that allowed the construction of personal (narrative) identity by establishing the continuities and discontinuities between the personal and collective spheres — according to Ricoeur's idea[46] — have been shaken. Tolerance has become, if we can call it that, a *gnoseological virtue*, a way of reaching the *I*, a possibility of a fresh encounter with our own fragility, with the radical artificiality we are made of. Tolerance, we might well say, provides an opportunity for a different identity.

Notes

1. Paul Virilio has made some interesting remarks on this at different times in his works. See *A Landscape of Events* (Cambridge, MA: MIT Press, 2000), where the subject is set in the wider framework of the transformations of the idea of history.
2. See also on this same topic the first two chapters, entitled "E la tolleranza una virú morale?" and "La tolleranza come virtú sociale e politica," from Anna Elisabetta Galeotti's book *La tolleranza. Una proposta pluralista* (Naples: Liguori Editore, 1994).
3. See, along the same line of argument, "Sobredosi de tolerància," in the journal *Generació*, Barcelona, no. 5, 1993.
4. The classic locus is G. W. F. Hegel, *The Science of Logic*, translated by W. H. Johnston and L. G. Struthers (London: George Allen & Unwin, 1929).
5. Not the first, as we know all too well. The German American anthropologist Franz Boas is usually regarded as the leading forerunner of cultural relativism, insofar as he opposes the postulates favorable to the unity of cultures and tries to demonstrate cultural pluralism comparatively. With him we should mention other authors, such as Herskovits or Alfred L. Kroeber, who in the 1930s and 1940s helped the development of this doctrine decisively, just as much more recently Clifford Geertz's

contributions have helped show the scope of a debate which overflows the bounds of the interests of cultural anthropologists.

6. In relation to both aspects, Todorov has made a pertinent observation: "the discourse of difference is a difficult one. What it risks is threatened by two dangers that seem to leave no room for a third way. According to the dominant ideology of our time, individualism, and its corollary, democracy, we start from an affirmation of equality which leads to an affirmation of identity: since men are equal everywhere, we refuse to recognize significant differences between them. We admit the differences, but then, carried along by the principle of identity itself, we translate them into terms of superiority and inferiority. We find it hard to accept that the other is simply another: we believe him, according to the case, to be worse or better, but always of the same race as ourselves." Tzvetan Todorov, "La conquista de México. Comunicación y encuentro de civilizaciones," a dialogue with Octavio Paz and Ignacio Bernal, *Claves de razón práctica*, no. 19, January–February 1992.

7. An approach proposed by Iring Fetscher in his book *Toleranz*, significantly subtitled *A Little Virtue Indispensable for Historical Democracy* (Stuttgart: Radius, 1990).

8. See *Toleranz*, the first chapters of which trace a brief historical panorama in which the different faces this notion has taken on in the past are indicated.

9. In particular his book *La barbarie: De ellos y de los nuestros* (Barcelona: Paidós, 1995).

10. Especially in his *Treatise on Toleration*. In the introduction to the Spanish translation (Madrid: Santillana, 1997) the editor, Roberto Rodríguez Aramayo, highlights the link between Voltaire's and Kant's ideas about cosmopolitanism when they say that only by feeling themselves to be citizens of the world above anything else can men one day eradicate wars from the face of the earth.

11. In his work "La tolerancia y lo intolerable," included in *Las morales de la historia* (Barcelona: Paidós, 1993, p. 178), Todorov quotes Montaigne's phrase taken from the essay "Of Vanity": "I look upon all men as my compatriots, and embrace a Polander as a Frenchman, preferring the universal and common tie to all national ties whatever."

12. At a moment like the present one, when so much is being said, mainly

because of Huntington's idea of the clash of civilizations, that distinction does not seem to be the most operative one. See Samuel P. Huntington, *The Clash of Civilizations: Remaking of the World Order* (New York: Simon & Schuster, 1996).

13. Although Ernesto Garzón Valdés has referred to this issue on many occasions, for the purposes of the present argument we should mention his work "Cinco confusiones acerca de la relevancia moral de la diversidad cultural," *Claves de Razón Práctica*, no. 74, July–August 1997, 10–23.

14. See "La tolerancia y lo intolerable," cit.

15. Referring to what he calls the "difficult question of the difference between men and women," Salvatore Veca has expounded a thesis structured in two parts: "a) policies and institutions must respond, for impersonal and neutral reasons, to *personal* differences and that is satisfied by the principle according to which treating equally is not equivalent to treating as equals; b) women as a collective identity or, if preferred, as a 'subject' who has struggled against other subjects to obtain recognition of 'autonomy' and equal dignity (of difference), enter the public discussion of citizenship, inevitably and mutually cooperative and conflictive, with their vocabularies of morality and redescriptions of the political and social world, with a repertory of dialogic competences, and this in turn is destined to generate a reclassification of life issues for women and men (citizens), a review of the *given* preferences which is not unconnected with a review of the given interpretations of differences" (Salvatore Veca, *Cittadinanza: Riflessioni filosofiche sull'idea di emancipazione*, Milan: Feltrinelli, 1990, pp. 94 et seq.).

16. That we are not arguing must in no event be interpreted as if we thought it of no importance. Arendt warned us of the gravity of that neglect: "No doubt, wherever public life and its law of equality are completely victorious, wherever a civilization succeeds in eliminating or reducing to a minimum the dark background of difference, it will end in complete petrification" (*The Origins of Totalitarianism*, London: Allen & Unwin, 1967, p. 302). Fina Birulés has used that quotation in her work "El sueño de la absoluta autonomía," in Amparo Gómez and Justine Tally (comps.), *La construcción social de lo femenino* (Santa Cruz de Tenerife: Centro de

Estudios de la Mujer de la Universidad de La Laguna-Instituto Canario de la Mujer, 1998).

17. Although many ancient and modern philosophers have striven to distinguish between the two senses of the word freedom, the most successful proposal is probably Isaiah Berlin's in his famous work *Two Concepts of Liberty* (Oxford: Clarendon Press, 1958). It also appears in a collection of his papers entitled *Four Essays on Liberty* (Oxford: Oxford University Press, 1969). See also Norberto Bobbio's book published as *Igualdad y libertad* (Barcelona: Paidós-ICE de la UAB, 1993), especially pp. 97 et seq.

18. See, for example, the way in which Geneviève Fraisse, in her work "Entre égalité et liberté," included in the collective volume *La Place des Femmes* (Paris: La Découverte, 1995), uses these categories to analyze the problem of women in developed Western societies, or Bobbio's treatment of the same distinction in his work *In Praise of Meekness*, translated by Teresa Chataway (Oxford: Wiley-Blackwell, 2000).

19. In his book *Equality and Partiality* (Oxford: Oxford University Press, 1991).

20. "Justice as Fairness" first appeared as an essay in 1959. Republished and expanded in *Justice as Fairness: A Restatement* (Cambridge, MA: Harvard University Press, 1999).

21. As Nagel points out, "liberalism purports to be a view that justifies religious toleration not only to religious skeptics, but to the devout, and sexual tolerance not only to libertines but to those who believe extramarital sex is sinful" (*Equality and Partiality*, cit.).

22. A subject Nagel has dealt with in detail in *The Possibility of Altruism* (Princeton, NJ: Princeton University Press, 1978).

23. The writer has set out his points of view in *On Toleration* (New Haven and London: Yale University Press, 1997).

24. This category demands a reference to Aurelio Arteta's book, *La compasión* (Barcelona: Paidós, 1996).

25. Gadamer more prudently prefers to put it the other way around: "tolerating the other in no way means losing full awareness of one's own vital essence" (*The Heritage of Europe*, 1989). See also *Praise of Theory: Speeches and Essays*, translated by Chris Dawson (New Haven, CT: Yale, 1999).

26. To pincers, family resemblances and other coincidences I referred
    in a newspaper article entitled "Todo vale (lo que vale)" (*El País*,
    December 27, 1997), which is included in the collection *A Diario*
    (Barcelona: Península, in print). That article was referred to by Helena
    Béjar in another text published in the same section (*El País*, August 1,
    1998), Fernando Broncano in his introduction to Feyerabend's book
    Ambigüedad y diferencia (Barcelona: Paidós, 1999, p. 33, note 21), set-
    ting out with sound arguments the suitability of regarding the author of
    Against Method as "one of us".

27. For a broad panorama of the most important contemporary conceptions
    of truth, see Juan Antonio Nicolás and Mª José Frápolli (eds), *Teorías de
    la verdad en el siglo XX* (Madrid: Tecnos, 1997).

28. Or, to put it more basically: "509. What I really want to say is that
    a language-game is only possible if one trusts something" (Ludwig
    Wittgenstein, *On Certainty*, compiled by G. E. M. Anscombe and G. H.
    von Wright, Oxford: Blackwell, 1969).

29. It can be no accident the thesis that there is exactly one true and complete
    description of the way the world is has been, as everyone knows, called
    by Putnam "a God's eye point of view".

30. See note 18.

31. Merton said: the same logic that affirms that the whites will never be able
    to understand the blacks because their life experience is radically different
    allows the affirmation that black Africans, who have not been through
    the experience of slavery, will never understand black Americans, but
    also maintains that the black Americans of the southern states will
    never understand those of the north, or say that black men will never
    understand black women, since they have undergone an added slavery,
    and so on. Perhaps the nuance we might bring to Merton's reasoning
    would lead us to delve even deeper into his perplexity, since where would
    the limit of this process of atomization be? In the individual? Or in his
    different moments or states?

32. This is undoubtedly one of the greatest misunderstandings fostered by
    Feyerabend's famous appeals to epistemological pluralism and toler-
    ance, appeals that have frequently been quoted in support by many
    critics of modern rationality. But Feyerabend's idea — quite worthy
    of consideration — requires a nuance if it is not to become a thesis

rendered useless by its excess. For pluralism and tolerance, valid for the pragmatic moment of rejection (even the most metaphysical of theories can bring critical benefits), cease to be significant values in the context of evaluation. We cannot yet see what a supposed evaluating tolerance might be, unless we regard it as merely turning a blind eye to the weaknesses of the theories, or a watering down of the criteria. But that — as Gustavo L. Marqués has rightly pointed out in his work "A propósito de la crítica de Feyerabend al racionalismo crítico" (*Sociedad Argentina de Análisis Filosófico* (SADAF), vol. 16, no. 1, May 1996, 17–26) — would amount to very much the same thing as "throwing out the baby with the bathwater."

33. Nagel, *Equality and Partiality*, cit.

34. Or the no less important error of thinking that with her affirmations the author of *Intention* is providing arguments to support those who believe that the world and its properties are no more than social constructions. That the stories of the world are produced by observers and are therefore relative to their capacities, education etc, does not affect the thesis that the world is real and independent of our perceptions. What is socially constructed is not the world or its properties but the vocabularies in the terms of which we know them.

35. Hilary Putnam had said something similar at several moments in his work. To give two examples, the chapters on Wittgenstein in *Renewing Philosophy* (Cambridge, MA: Harvard University Press, 1992) or his analysis of relativism in chapter 5 of *Reason, Truth, and History* (Cambridge: Cambridge University Press, 1981).

36. The same idea is expressed another way, no less forceful for those alluded to in the end. We can, like Stanley Cavell in his book *The Claim of Reason* (Oxford: Oxford University Press, 1979), point out that both the expectation that there is a great metaphysical solution to all our problems and the skeptical, relativist or nihilistic getaway are different symptoms of the same disease. The disease of being incapable of accepting the world and other people or, as he says in the text, "to acknowledge the world and to acknowledge other people, without the guarantees."

37. Miguel Angel Quintanilla used that exact adjective to specify his philosophical position. In his introduction to the translation of Putnam's book *The Many Faces of Realism* (Barcelona: Paidós, 1994), he points out

that one merit of the tentative realism he proposes is to have discovered that the concept of partial and incomplete truth may be of fundamental importance for our philosophical image of the world and our place in it ("in the end, in everyday life — and still less in the science laboratory — we rarely use the idea of absolute, complete truth").

38. Ludwig Wittgenstein, *On Certainty*. For Wittgenstein's position on this question see also the work by Nicolás Sánchez Durá, "Miradas fulgurantes y traductores caritativos," in J. Marrades Millet and N. Sánchez Durá (comps.), *Mirar con cuidado* (Valencia: Pre-textos, 1994). Vicente Sanfélix made a few observations to me on this subject that have been useful for this exposition.

39. For example, Saul Kripke in his *Wittgenstein: Reglas y lenguaje privado* (Mexico: Instituto de Investigaciones Filosóficas-UNAM, 1989).

40. For many interpreters, as is the case with the feminist scholar Linda Nicholson, the philosophical position that has assumed this attitude most decidedly is postmodernity: "the more radical move in the postmodern turn was to claim that the very criteria demarcating the true and the false, as well as such related distinctions as science and myth or fact and superstition, were internal to the traditions of modernity and could not be legitimized outside of those traditions" (introduction to her compilation *Feminism/Postmodernism*, New York: Routledge, 1990, p. 4).

41. See also Manuel Fraijó's work "Relativismo y religión," in L. Arenas, J. Muñoz and A. J. Perona (comps.), *El desafío del relativismo* (Madrid: Trotta, 1997, pp. 163–82), which argues in favor of a relativism compatible with religious belief — that is, defends Christianity as true but not absolutely.

42. Since the question is not central to what we are dealing with here, this one reference will suffice: E. Lévinas, *Difficile liberté* (Paris: Albin Michel, 3rd ed. corrected and expanded, 1995), where the question of the nexus between religious tolerance and freedom is alluded to in different passages.

43. Therefore, there is nothing in his premises that prevents him from taking pluralist positions. Quite the opposite, he thinks that it is the relativist who is in no theoretical condition to assume those positions to the end. For a complete, attentive reconstruction of this issue, though from a

point of view that does not always coincide with the one developed here, see León Olivé's book *Multiculturalismo y pluralismo* (Mexico: Paidós, 1999).

44. Francisco Fernández Buey has talked about this, not in relation to the past but from the perspective of the present, in the book, written in association with Jorge Riechmann, *Ni tribunos*, (Madrid: Siglo XXI, 1996), especially the section "Atención a lo prepolítico," pp. 107–9.

45. Accepting the definition of the category traditionally attributed to Aristotle, according to whom contingency is everything that is not necessary or impossible.

46. Or Taylor's, to mention another author with a similar idea. See his well-known work "The Politics of Recognition" in Charles Taylor, Steven Rockefeller, Michael Walzer, Susan Wolf, Amy Gutmann, *Multiculturalism: Examining The Politics of Recognition* (Princeton, NJ: Princeton University Press, 1994).

Epilogue: The Insomniac's Meditation

What a strange disturbance is this emerging into an unknown region of awareness. Suddenly, for no reason, the peaceful journey of rest is interrupted. A rough hand tears the wrapping of the night. We are in a darkness inhabited by ghosts and fears, memories and passions, where everything is a piece of incontestable evidence: the desire that surprises and the horror that paralyzes, the unmentionable in wakefulness and the lingering recollection. We are seized by fear or overwhelmed by tedium, by definition always infinite. "Here is an intensity with no escape," the insomniac thinks. The whole world of wakefulness is in brackets. All stimuli have faded away, with the objects we usually apply ourselves to. Nothing in reality attracts our attention, nothing tugs at us. Life suspended in the air, in the dark, in the void. Perfectly useless, like some old idea.

Bodies lie, abandoned to their fate, yielding to the cadence of nature, the monotony of cycles, making the rhythm of things their own. There is scarcely a breath to be heard. Defenselessness of the sleeper. It is easy to feel solidarity with him, even though he exudes an uncompromising hint of strangeness. Let us stop wondering what he is thinking about and scan his face: what is he dreaming about? The insomniac is distracted and concocts a Borgesian diversion. Dreams communicate with one another: we intervene in the dreams of famous people, but they do not register our presence (as we do theirs) because they do not know us. We are the set, the props, of their dreams. Until one day the secret weft that connects minds comes to light. We are introduced to one of them and he says: "Haven't we met before?" As in the film we live in a great city, noisy and disorderly, that is connected by the rooftops.

But now it is not in our hands to decide what we are going to think. The poet's statement has been working on its own account for days: "memory is obscene." Only now do we understand that he was right. Our whole life passes before us, as in the imminence of death, as they say. An excessive, overwhelming referent we rarely come into contact with, perhaps because we fear the encounter, because we step back in the face of what we sense will be the marshy, stormy spectacle of our interior (Kafka). Perhaps the function of all that more or less conventional repertory of stories about what has become of us so far and what we believe we can hope for is to sidetrack us from this object, to postpone the confrontation with ourselves until the last possible moment.

The regulation 20 years soon passes, just as the age when memory becomes a low buzz of birthdays soon arrives. It would be a mistake to take that for nostalgia, a mere yearning for what is lost. Knowledge is expressed in many ways; one special way is that counterpoint between times, that constant meditation of the distances between yesterday and today, before and now, that makes us know about ourselves and the world, the true nature of our projects and the stubborn resistance of events. The tension with the past only matters if it sheds light on our present or, to put it another way, if it helps us to know ourselves better. *What there is now* is valued from expectations that, almost by definition, come from behind, were shaped in the past. A past that seems to be winning battles after death: the same battles it was incapable of winning when it was the present.

Perhaps there is an important key to the way we relate to our today in that imbalance. A bad business putting the cart before the horse, and raw reality, always imperfect and disappointing, after the ideals. Utopia cannot reside in the past. After utopia there is only room for failure, for when utopia disappears the very possibility of continuing to think about our future in terms of a process determined by ends disappears with it. With the loss of hopes men also lose all sense of direction. They are disappointed and confused. This is not a new situation; now we can understand (instead of declaring our absolute astonishment at them) how those who discovered the monstrous face of a cause they had believed to be just lived their past, how they perceived their particular historical circumstance. But their dream had a substance, a texture, a density of experience that ours did not. It was a dream that ran anxiously in search of life. In that way, unawares, they made the sociologist's ambiguous diagnosis come true: utopia, which at one time completely transcended history, tends to become more like real life.

For us the same terms are not valid, but the general principle may be. *What there was* must be a reference but not a model. Only in that way shall we be safe from that state of mind so characteristic of recent years: being permanently on the point of disillusion, disenchantment. The model is crushing in its perfection, and many people obtain some strange satisfaction from defeat. It is not worth lingering too long over clarifying the nature of that satisfaction. It seems like the sad, empty victory of consistency: people perfectly adapted to their reality and equally freed from all enthusiasm. Their adolescent satisfaction at *being adults* needed something to abandon or something to abandon them, and at last they have found it. It is, as Mannheim would have said, the triumph of the "positive and practical" attitude [*Sachlichkeit*] that, when all is said and done, means the decadence of human will. But that is not the natural function of the model: the ideal is to help us get out of reality, not live it like a jail sentence. The memory of the past, on the other hand, should serve to let us know ourselves better. The way we are and the way we were. And so that distant consideration of ethics and politics that some people put forward ("without ethics there is no politics; there is only politicking") in fact described nothing; it confined itself to pointing to a *desideratum*, a horizon of values that, despite everything, we are a little closer to now. The reality of now has to be compared with the reality of then, just as the ideals of today have to be seen against the light of those of that time. Crossing terms leads inexorably to confusion, and we should not think clearly about the future without having put our relations with the past in order. What happens does not always *teach*: on occasion its meaning depends on the present. We should not be deceived by the irreversible character of what has happened: there were mistakes in the past too.

This perspective will be the right one if it allows us to show all the indeterminacy of the present or, far better, if it allows us to free all the *possibility* it contains. Now that its failure in other territories has been consummated, utopia can then be retrieved to carry out that task of exploring the possible, of delving into what someone called the *lateral possibilities of reality*. It may have turned out to be true that demanding the impossible is the best way of being realistic. Indeed, Max Weber had already told us: "To attain the possible one has to reach out for the impossible." But to commit oneself to the non-enclosed character of the world implies a supposition, the existence of a sphere that houses that process, an entity that makes the fulfillment of expectations its own. Why do we not continue to call it subject or identity? But ideas associate by themselves and the doubt arises: how to describe an idea of that kind? The insomniac, a philosopher in the end, recalls the formulation of the *hard* principles of metaphysics presented some time ago by Vattimo, and breathes easier: *subject* as the fundamental entity of meaning, *object* as the stable reference of thought, *reason* as the hierarchical device of the submission of the latter to the needs of the former, and *technique* as a consummated manifestation of its triumph in the form of total control of reality. The identity and subject he is thinking of neither have those features nor accomplish that mission. He thinks, with Arendt,[1] of a subject that is resolved at two major moments: birth and death. The birth of each individual is the promise of a new beginning; acting means being capable of taking initiatives and doing the unexpected. A new being is the supreme example of *what takes time to show its meaning*: he takes his whole life. On the other hand, death means not only ceasing to know but also, most of all, ceasing to dream — that is, to anticipate, to plan. It is the moment when the individual at last finds his regulatory idea.[2] Two moments between which the entire arc of human life is drawn. Identity cannot claim to be a firm place either.

Indeed, one has the impression that even the defense of a plurality of identities as opposed to the old monolithic one is about to become an anachronism. Some sociologists have warned of that and probably the fascination of more than one European philosopher with the United States has to do with that, among other things. In order to function, that old use of identity required a persistence of presence and its reflection that are no longer the case. A certain degree (or rhythm?) of labor mobility, for example, prevents individuals from seeking their signs of identity in work. Something similar happens if they look at other spheres, such as personal relations, where any form of perpetuity has disappeared from the horizon. The model being proposed to these men to represent themselves is one of those multipurpose toys that start out as a car but can be turned into a thousand different artifacts just by assembling the same pieces in another way.

Faced with a reality like that, there does not seem to be room for many alternatives. The one some contemporary authors have defended is that for individuals to survive in these conditions they have to abandon themselves to a rapid fragmentation of the *I*, obeying logics of all kinds and living a process of desublimation, fleeing from sentiment and sentimentalism, hiding in short from any social vulnerability. The Wittgenstein of *Philosophical Investigations* is usually good for elaborating that point. Once the subject is rejected ("the subject is a product of the representation machine and disappears with it," Lyotard wrote in the early 1970s), all that remains is to defend a nonnegotiable pluralism of language games and heighten the nonnegotiable local character of all discourses, agreements and legitimizations. The idea has a greater scope than it might appear at first glance, since we should not forget that for Wittgenstein language games are ways of life. They are sets of linguistic and nonlinguistic activities, institutions, practices and meanings embodied in them. It is not by chance that those who defend a *weak* conception of the world (based on discussion, respect for plurality and the emancipation of men from the structures of power) have thought that in the later Wittgenstein they have found an occasional reinforcement for some of their postulates.

But in that characterization of a *weak* identity (almost *in retreat*) a key element is missing. It is neither forgetting nor neglect, but necessary absence. On occasion personalizing ideas fulfills a clarifying function, similar to that of giving examples: whoever longs for a time when everything seemed possible because everything was still to be done is the inverted, parodic correlate of the person who maintains, distorting language and contra Wittgenstein,[3] that there is no need to do anything more than what is being done. A common anachronism with a different date: an identical rejection of history. The officially stamped self-satisfaction of those who hold power and the self-punishment of the eternally dissatisfied each in their own way represent similar diseases of memory. They are both managing to live without goals (irremediably lost), without meaning or deep commitment.

It is not a matter of stepping back in fright from this conclusion: there is nothing to fear in the field of thought. It is more a question of deciding *which ideas we want to live with*. That identity to which we assigned the task of exploring the possible derives its main symbols not only from our present and our past but also from what we hope for in the future. Our identity is a weak identity, because its definition includes an unavoidable element of indeterminacy. Nobody knows what the future holds for us, individually or collectively. But that *not yet* is both awaited and desired. It will occur to a large extent if we are open to new situations and provide the means for them to happen. What we are (both what we say we are and what we think we are) is also constituted by what we hope to be but are not yet. Utopia returns to inscribe itself on the heart of that always suspended identity.

But the insomniac thinks he sees clearly inside the discovered darkness. It is true that a certain kind of fulfillment can only be achieved in a time perspective, when individuals recognize the instant as the result-foretaste of the past-future. Living in time but without memory and without commitment is like settling into a deceitful *as if*. It is the wrong way of affirming oneself. I even wrote that some time ago: there is something inert about a reality without subjects. It is they who activate it, they who give it life. If they fail to do so, the horizon of the entire world is shrouded in melancholy. One can feel the temptation to put the blame on knowledge, as Nietzsche does in the second of his *Untimely Meditations*, "On the Use and Abuse of History for Life." Ramón Llull had already spoken of *sadness for superabundance of thought*, and in his engraving *Melancholia* Dürer seems to be trying to capture that same experience, of the one *who knows too much* (of the one who *does not dare to know*, as a man of the Enlightenment would have said). But it was Benjamin who managed to understand it as the trace — the memory — of the absent subject: "the melancholic sees with terror that the earth is returning to a merely natural state, it exhales no breath of history, no aura." Silence is the *speechless name* of sadness. It is memory that originally feeds the desire for fulfillment for the present. The problem, the great problem that arises at this point, is that all the statements listed so far appeal to an experience that seems to have mutated during the night.

The past that is emerging now is not the same as the one that exists in wakefulness. From the episodes that have managed to cross the wilderness of oblivion and have returned in their insolent freshness to remind us of the persistence of an *I* we believed definitively buried, to new tonalities for everything that never left awareness. Happy childhood? Anguished adolescence? Was there ever fulfillment? In which stretch of the life already lived did we lay the foundations of this present? Is there anything worth missing? Nothing is as it is in the light of day and, most seriously, nothing in this recollection seems to depend on us. Involuntary memory or dependence on another will, an unknown will? The old stories, those narratives that seemed to recount what had happened to us so far, and which we based our hopes for the future on, are revealed at this instant as an artificial convention, a fallacious construction that breaches the most elementary rules of the game. A stupid player cheating himself. Or it may be something else. Perhaps the poor wretch does not know what he is holding, or the scope of the bet.

Like the angel, the insomniac gazes at the rubble of his own life. Unlike Klee's, his gaze does not reflect horror. It must be — he thinks aloud — that repetition has finally made us a little wise, and we have learned what must be done in these situations. There is a first certainty to cling to: only language allows us to have positive dealings with experience, to escape from the enclosure of the given and start along the path to knowledge. It is true that on occasions the intensity of a particular experience may push us to silence, seem to favor our private tendency to remain dumb. The question is whether from a place like that we can reach a different conclusion from the one proposed by the old philosophies of life — that is, reactivate a precategorical state in which an *aeterna veritas* can occur. Benjamin was also extremely mistrustful of any kind of refuge in the merely *lived*. Hence his fascination with Proust or Kafka. In their works both writers embody the attempt to make it possible to convey experience in the contemporary world again (even, in the case of Kafka, at the price of renouncing the truth). Benjamin's attitude overlaps in this case, as in so many others, with Wittgenstein's: where he proposes to rage against the limits of language, claw back land from the ocean of everything that cannot be spoken of, Benjamin defends the need to "make the territories in which only madness has grown so far cultivable; penetrate with the sharp axe of reason without looking to right or left so as not to fall a victim to the horror that beckons from the depths of the primordial jungle."

It may not be much to begin with — there should be no serious problem admitting it. Benjamin himself, who praises the Cartesian breaking gesture of making a *tabula rasa* of the past, admits that all those who have decided to "start from scratch" have been obliged to get by with very little, "to build from little." But there is something ironic about that modesty. For that little we have to start from, which we try to capture with our language, is that fleeting imaginary reality that flashes at the instant of involuntary memory. A reality in which we can find those Proustian jewels of *another experience*, completely different from the one offered by usual intelligence. Reinforcements to overcome the initial perplexities have arrived. At a first moment that whole *novum* that has just irrupted into awareness is perceived as disorder — as disorder and as destruction. For the logic that introduces that new remembered experience is the logic of discontinuity. The angel, at least in this, was mistaken: the idea of the *continuum* does not sweep everything away. Now we see that it is possible to interrupt the inexorable linearity of classic time and accede to a different image of the present and the future.

In a way, the roles are reversed this time. It is not we who have traveled to *what has already been* in search of a reaffirmation of what there is now, or a sickly sweet consolation that will relieve the hardships of our present; it is the past that has come to put pressure on us, which has appeared before our eyes to ask to be freed. The point is to rescue and redeem a past that has been defeated and condemned to the darkness of madness or oblivion. To make a place for it in our present and provide it with meaning is thus the task awaiting completion: "forgetting is inhuman because the accumulated suffering is forgotten; for the trace of history on things, colors and sounds is always the trace of past suffering" (Adorno). The word "history" has not slipped in here by chance, nor has the language of antagonism been lightly introduced. For what has kidnapped that past, what keeps it confined in the nocturnal, malign depths of our being, is an order that comes from outside, the order that controls the present and the past. The culture of the dominators, in short.

We can say this without abandoning the first person. That kidnapped world that seeks the light can be glimpsed fleetingly through experiences, objects or situations that are absolutely its own. Into the personal events revived in individual memory creep the anxieties and yearnings of humanity, the general in the particular. Fragments beloved of childhood and despised by the culture and knowledge of adults, lost desires, forbidden impulses, futile aspirations or impossible flights . . . all elements that are hard for the comfortable subject of the vigil to assume. This recollection of the past stirs up dangerous prospects: the established order is suspicious of the subversive contents of memory. Perhaps those were the reasons that led Benjamin to think that the subject of the new experience can only be an alternative to the subject of the dominion of the bourgeois reason in power. We must not be confused by the fact that this terminology may sound a trifle anachronistic today. Things can be expressed another way and then Benjamin's conviction becomes less anachronistic, or more likely. The supposed alternative subject does not aspire to found an alternative macroknowledge. On the contrary, precisely because he attempts to incorporate the experience of precarious- ness, of expiry, his is a knowledge *in suspense*, a knowledge that by definition cannot aspire to any kind of eternity. It would be a good deal if that subject were capable of moving in his present, in the new present involuntary that memory has just provided him with. For that he has to abandon both the fascination of the future and the rigidly causal image of the past or, in the language of the philosophy of history, both faith in progress and the aspiration to unitary historical reconstruction that, applied to his own life, produces an image of himself that has ended up being a genuine obstacle to (self-)knowledge.

Suddenly, in the midst of that reflection, a conversation with a friend crops up: is memory something that one has or something that has been lost? Who knows, he thought at that time. We only know that the effort to remember often ends in sadness. Could it be that we like being sad then? Perhaps so and, the insomniac wanders off again, should we apply the *paradox of the masochist*,[4] which he may have stated in terms of the question: does he go to heaven or hell? (The development is easy to imagine: if he goes to heaven, where he does not suffer, he is suffering because he is not suffering, but if he is sent to hell, and he likes pain, he is enjoying it, and so it is also difficult to see where the punishment is. A tight corner for the Supreme Judge, from which he could escape by arguing, for example, that God rewards and punishes *à la carte*.) This is only half a joke, the insomniac realizes. The Nietzsche who is the enemy of memory and advocate of forgetting as the supreme life faculty rejected attempts to understand the continuity of history in the sense of the history of remembered suffering as masochistic.

The *half a joke* has distracted him for an instant from the thread of the meditation (although he may well have gained from the digression). He has shown the theoretical suitability of distinguishing between two different memories. Because the pain caused by remembering past (and thus lost) happiness is not the same as the memory of past suffering, insofar as it is witness to an unfulfilled happiness (and insofar as one still aspires to it). Perhaps with that difference we could cross the demarcation line between *qualities of memory*, perhaps in the different materials with which each of them operates, the particular efficacy of the entities exterior to the subject is revealed. In the face of the memory coated with the clay of linear time we have the experience of the instant at the moment of danger. In the face of the mistaken historicist conviction that the creation of memory moves at the pace of history, there is the will to catch the conflict in the act. Reality is a dead end (or a one-way street, if you prefer). We have just introduced an irreversible suspicion, that the experience of history does not coincide with the presence of history. While we do not know how history happens to us, history happens. Memory is only one of the faces of the past.

That is why the silent terror of the angel is a gesture to escape from. His face shows the impotence of the limit, a limit the content of which, as Franco Rella suggests,[5] can be expressed through Zarathustra's tragic paradox: the impossible *loving backward*. A love of fragments, salvaged in their condition as traces to be deciphered, is not enough. The collector's love of the singular object or of a collection of objects is not enough, like that childhood that appears as the space of possible redemption. Modern archivists, who collect historical objects, removed from the homogeneous chain of time, but also removed from any meaning for the subject, are prey to what Benjamin would call the magic of the trace, trapped in the spell of the fragment, astonished by the artificiality. No knowledge can spring from there, only (who would have though it!) mere philology, a magical fixation on the object that it is up to philosophy to exorcize. The exorcism does not mean despising the particular, from which on principle one should draw a *presumption of truth*, but showing what is merely conviction.

To do so it is necessary to construct *the mirror that reflects a new reality*, a new relation with the world, with things, even with one's own body. The moment of destruction, represented by the experience of the instant of involuntary memory, is not enough to free the past, to allow it to lose its condition of a trophy of the conquerors. With all that heap of rubble that precedes us and pursues us, with that pile of ruins that rises unstoppably toward the sky, it is possible to have a relationship other than that of the angel's desperate, sterile love. Once and for all, from such events we must produce knowledge. Benjamin's words now express to perfection that knowledge people aspire to: "History in the strict sense is [. . .] an image that originates in the involuntary memory, an image which in the second of danger appears unexpectedly to the subject of history." Therefore, it is not a totality we must have direct dealings with; it is, rather, a promise to be pursued.

There is no terror in the insomniac's gaze, which does not mean that he steps back from any of the horrors of the past. He also believes that, like the angel, he has caught a glimpse of disasters where the dominant reason tries to convince us that there is continuity and progress, but does not believe that he should be silent in the face of the possibility of recomposing what has been destroyed. When all is said and done, from what has already been thought we cannot identify this task with any more or less concealed way of restoring the old order. The sharp eye of knowledge of the crisis, which for Benjamin is the historian's eye, perceives in the mutilated character of the past the condition of possibility for the emergence of new figures, new images, through which the one who has been silenced can begin to speak again. The knowledge that from all this things can be developed must be a knowledge of emergency and precariousness, but knowledge nevertheless. Naturally, it cannot take the same shape as other kinds of knowledge that have also proposed the intelligibility of humanity. But this whole reflection began by affirming the central place of memory — that is, its condition as the *essential note of the finite and historical being of man* (Gadamer). By shunning any possible reduction to a psychological faculty, at the same time we distance ourselves from the obligatory corollary of this attitude, which is none other than scientism. The abstract contrast between history as a mere memory and history as a science also comes inexorably to a dead end in which, on the one hand, we have a memory that has become ineffable or placed in the hands of the psychologists and, on the other, a history rationally classified in the computer database where, by definition, there is no room for forgetting or remembering.

The knowledge of history, the insomniac begins to suspect, must be a knowledge of a new kind: a new knowledge at the service of another experience. But we do not find that knowledge made or given anywhere; on the contrary, we have to construct it from the materials supplied by the involuntary memory. Soon the old words are no use as they are. Ordinary speech, which shows lies, precariousness, uncertainty, contains the traces of a wealth that must be conquered if we wish to reappropriate the world. The combat is fraught with dangers. Memory, Benjamin warned us, can also be a "deadly game." What it gives us are *hieroglyphics* to be interpreted, intense qualitative aggregates awaiting the intellectual construction where they can show their meaning. Sensations are not data, but *signs of other laws and ideas*, just as memories do not refer to events in the past, at least understood as cancelled realities ("what science takes as *established* can be altered by memory," Benjamin).

But nor does it seem that the old genres can be very useful once we have radically reconsidered the meaning of the terms at stake. It is the rejection of a certain idea that led Cioran to write:

> The luck the novelist or the dramatist has is to express himself in disguise, to free himself of his conflicts and, even more, of all those characters that fight within him . . . The essayist, on the other hand, is trapped in a thankless genre, where only his own incompatibilities are projected, contradicting one another at every step.

Whereas the discovery of the nature of the historical picture as a picture of lights and shadows, reliefs and omissions, memories and forgettings, leads Benjamin, concerned with finding a way to translate those images into knowledge, to wonder: "what could it consist of if not creating 'a work of art'?"

Identity and knowledge have met once again, and it could not be any other way. The place of that new meeting has been that particular Benjamin idea of subjectivity, that rare mixture of determinations of knowledge and action that is sometimes called the *storyteller* and sometimes the *historian*, and which might be unified under the label the *historian who tells stories.* "Storytelling is not just an art; it is a kind of dignity — if not in the East an office. *It culminates in wisdom*, just as, for its part, wisdom often substantiates itself as story," we can read in his short story *The Handkerchief.* But as wisdom it seems to be a wisdom in peril in the world of today. We might say that it has seized from us a power we thought could not be taken away, absolutely firm: the power to *exchange experiences*, power that for Benjamin is exercised in exemplary fashion by authors like Kafka or Proust. The least of it is that in a strictly corporative sense they were not *professional historians* (if someone were to pose the issue in those terms one would have to ask him: who has helped us more than them to understand our time?). What matters is whether there are indications or examples of a different way of relating to the world in their texts or, which comes to the same thing, if they show us that *other* knowledge we are thinking of in action. In the end, the historian should be the same as any other writer here. The difference, if any, might lie in the fact that while for the historian forgetting himself — his particular circumstance, his specific moment — is a condition for the encounter with the past, for the other it is the guarantee of his future projection. But the difference is delicate, perhaps because it is insufficient. The historian's act of understanding is sent back toward the future in the hope that someone there will take charge of its content. The bad historian talks about himself (albeit in spite of himself) instead of assuming the condition of a vehicle for understanding. The same thing happens with the poet. Insofar as poetry is always linked to the personal circumstance of the person writing it, it has to some extent been regarded as a confidence. However, *great poetry* is the kind in which tradition speaks, the language speaks. The author disappears and the text remains. The poem is transformed into a *confidence of the language itself*. None of that is an attempt to deny identity, but to point out its expiry or its sphere of validity, as you like. Hermann Broch said of himself and of Musil and Kafka: "We are writers without a real biography. We have lived and we have written. That is all." Of course they had eventful existences (we need only think of Broch). That is not the question. The question is whether they attribute meaning to what happened to them or whether they want to disappear behind their work. Curious: it is that innocent, modest figure that is in danger, it is the incipient, fledgling knowledge that offers us what seems to be systematically denied us. There is nothing random about these facts. They undoubtedly have to do with a fundamental feature of the fact of storytelling: its orientation toward practical interest. The repeated Nietszchean dictate according to which each person "reaches the degree of truth he is able to bear" could obtain the counterpoint of Isak Dinesen's statement that so drew the attention of Arendt: "all sorrows can be borne if you put them into a story or tell a story about them." The storyteller is someone who wants to be useful, who wants to make his capacity for giving advice available to others. Morals, practical hints, proverbs or rules of life are other such forms, Benjamin would say, of advising the listener. The storyteller takes what he tells of the experience, whether his own or someone else's, and remakes it into the experience of those who listen to his story. There is no possibility of interpreting Dinesen's quotation in maliciously consoling terms: the very act of recounting the sorrow is insufferable for power, which would like to condemn the sufferer to oblivion, to a definitive nonexistence.

Without saying so, that act also introduces a valuation of the great inher-ited stories. The little stories are subversive because they unmask the lie of the Great Story — that is, everything that had been buried or discarded, falsified or forgotten. But that those who have never spoken speak now, that what so far had been silenced is said or that our own memory perturbs us are still only premises awaiting a framework of meaning to integrate them. If we do not find it we shall be lost in pure destructive gesture, in the angel's impossible love of the rubble, the fragments and the traces. The positive sense of the idea is inscribed in Benjamin's own terms: "the plurality of History is similar to the plurality of languages; universal history as practised since the nineteenth century can never have been more than a kind of Esperanto." In view of that, the defense of an integral prose, a language equal to the perception of history as "a plurality of histories" is no longer merely programmatic; it is an exact consequence of the suppositions advanced. The search for that global horizon is the task of the historian. More precisely, of what Benjamin called the *materialist historian.*

But let us not allow this language of horizons and tasks to take us toward images that are definitely not the case. We were warned against that by Marx, no less, who saw revolutions as "the locomotives of universal history" (when they might be "the lever of the handbrake on the train of travelling humanity"). Likewise the materialist historian is not that docile *civil servant of the present*, entirely devoted to updating the past — in other words, to interpreting it from the most complete interiorization of the categories of the logic of power. To regard what is given as obvious is a way, particularly effective since it is invisible, of reinforcing the conquerors' point of view. To understand the past empathetically can only be done from a subjectivity that is itself a historical and social construction (and is normally not known to be such). The alternative is, rather, to be found close to the humble description of herself (again) made by Dinesen when she wrote: "I am a storyteller and nothing more. It is the story itself that interests me and the way of telling it." Someone, to put it another way, who knows that her destiny is to be a vehicle for a new experience, an involuntary opportunity for us to be able to breathe, if only fleetingly, "a breath of that air breathed by those who have gone before us" (Simone Weil).

Perhaps, rather than *weak* identity we should speak of *impending* or *postponed* identity. Because what is at stake in that battle for the oppressed past, of which the historian becomes the chronicler, is precisely the very possibility of hope or "only thanks to those without hope have we been given hope." The unfulfilled dreams of the men of the past reveal the imposture of the present, shed new light on the reality we are immersed in. Who thinks in terms of salvation? The providentialist conception of history, messianism, is an avoidable theoretical danger. Of course, the presumption of a past without an end and without closure does not mean that the dead can be brought back to life. Past injustice is past and over. There will be no last judgment to redeem the suffering — only the religious thinker can expect that. Thought can never justify expectations of that kind. Need and despair are not forms of logical validity, Witzenmann observed, not without a certain cynicism. A century and a half later Horkheimer hit the same nail on the head: "Is monstrosity a convincing argument against the affirmation or denial of a state of affairs? Does logic have a law to the effect that a judgement is false when its consequence is despair?" There is only one figure and one attitude opposed to that of the religious thinker: "the materialist allows himself to be steeped in the feeling of the unlimited abandonment of humanity, which is the only true response to hope of the impossible." Can we not go farther than that? Does truth condemn us to silence? Perhaps everything revolves around a nuance: the plea of those who suffered cannot be dealt with, but their voice must be heard. To redeem is not to revive, nor to retrace one's steps: it is to provide access to meaning. Tenacity has led to a new question. For once that feeling of abandonment referred to by Horkheimer has pervaded us, what can we do with men's longing to live in a different world?

Tiredness is beginning to lay hold of the insomniac. At this stage of the night he cannot avoid the feeling that the discourse has been drifting away from the initial stimulus. Slippery as ever, slippery as mercury, the original object is beginning to escape: life itself. He wanted it to be the regulatory idea and it has ended up becoming the horizon of his unease, the dark cause of his disquiet. He remembers the words of Yourcenar he had read a few hours earlier: "Why is there not a single body so that I can embrace it, a single fruit so that I can cut it and a single enigma so that I can solve it in the end . . ." He feels lost in an ungraspable territory, the confines of which are barely marked. The flash of lightning has darkened; the involuntary memory is fading. He is afraid of being left with the old referents of wakefulness (usual experience, ordinary language, common sense . . .) the efficacy of which is well known to him. Now he realizes that what Benjamin had presented as a procedure is in fact a challenge: "to live through the Past with the intensity of a dream, in order to experience the present as the waking world that dream relates to." But he is worried about the danger of voluntarism: do the slogans of those who went before him really serve as the foundations of his action?

And if the answer is no, from where can he value that estrangement? There are no models, true, for the person who does not know the face of what he is searching for. How easy it is now to understand what Benjamin wrote to Scholem on March 14, 1939: "The stimuli the world today offers me are too weak, and the rewards of the future world too uncertain." But there may still be a greater truth, on the very edge of what we can bear. The one expressed by Octavio Paz when he wrote: "Whoever has seen hope does not forget it. And he dreams that one day he will find it again among his own."

Notes

1. The insomniac seems to be referring to his text "Hannah Arendt, pensadora del siglo," *Introducción a Hannah Arendt, La condición humana* (Barcelona: Paidós, 1993), although it is also possible that he is referring to M. Cruz and F. Birulés (eds), *En torno a Hannah Arendt* (Madrid: Centro de Estudios Constitucionales, 1994).

2. Elias Canetti has written: "Death is the first and oldest, one would even be tempted to say: the only fact. It is of a monstrous age and yet new every hour. Its degree of hardness is ten, and it also cuts like a diamond. It has the absolute cold of outer space, minus 273°. It has the wind speed of a hurricane, the highest. It is the very real superlative, of everything, but it is not infinite, for it is reached by every path. So long as death exists, any light is a will-of-the-wisp, for it leads to it. So long as death exists, no beauty is beauty, no goodness is goodness" (Elias Canetti, *The Conscience of Words*, translated by Joachim Neugroschel, London: André Deutsch, 1986, pp. 6–7).

3. Who wrote: "Everything we see could also be otherwise."

4. In a way complementary to the hedonist paradox that can be illustrated by Hobbes's anecdote referred to in John Aubrey's *Brief Lives*: "One time, I remember, going into the Strand, a poor and infirm old man craved his alms. He beholding him with eyes of pity and compassion, put his hand in his pocket, and gave him 6d. Said a divine (that is Dr Jasper Mayne) that stood by — 'Would you have done this, if it had not been Christ's command?' 'Yes,' said he. 'Why?' said the other. 'Because,' said he, 'I was in pain to consider the miserable condition of the old man; and now

my alms, giving him some relief, doth also ease me.'" The anecdote is quoted in A. MacIntyre, "Egoism and Altruism," in P. Edwards (ed.), *Encyclopedia of Philosophy* (New York: Macmillan & Free Press/London: Collier-Macmillan, 1967, vols 1–2), pp. 462–6/p. 463.

5. Doubtless the insomniac is referring to the book *Il silenzio e le parole* (Milan: Feltrinelli, 5th ed. 1987). The third chapter contains a brilliant analysis of Benjamin's work.

Index

Adorno, T. W. 79, 110
Annan, K. 5
Anscombe, E. 86, 98n. 28
Apel, K.-O. 56n. 11
Arendt, H. 21-6, 28n. 2, 29n. 7, 29n. 16,
    30n. 18, 30n. 21, 56n. 15, 65, 96n. 16, 106,
    115, 118n. 1
Aristotle, 101n. 45
Arteta, A. 97n. 24
Aubrey, J. 118n. 4
Austin, J. L. 79

Barcellona, P. 66n. 1
Baudelaire, C. 13
Béjar, H. 98n. 26
Benjamin, W. 13, 39, 65, 108-10, 112-18,
    119n. 5
Berger, P. 57n. 25
Bergson, H. 56n. 16
Berlin, I. 97n. 17
Birulés, F. 57n. 25, 96n. 16, 118n. 1
Boas, F. 94n. 5
Bobbio, N. 97n. 17, 97n. 18
Borges, J. L. 61
Brauer, D. 56n. 10
Broch, H. 115
Broncano, F. 98n. 26
Bruckner, P. 30n. 17

Camps, V. 30n. 22
Canneti, E. 56n. 9, 118n. 2
Cavell, S. 99n. 36

Chebel d'Appollonia, A. 7
Cioran, E. 114
Collingwood, R. G. 85
Crusoe, R. 35
Cruz, M. 55n. 4, 55n. 6, 118n. 1

Dal Lago, A.
Davidson, D. 55n. 2
Delgado, M. 7
Derrida, J. 56n. 13
Dinesen, I. 115-16
Donne, J. 58
Dotti, J. 56n. 14
Dürer, A. 108

Enzensberger, H. M. 18-19, 21, 28n. 4
Esposito, R. 55n. 5, 57n. 22
Even-Granboulan, G. 30n. 21

Férnandez Buey, F. 76, 101n. 44
Ferry, L. 16
Fetscher, I. 82-3, 95n. 7
Feyerabend, P. 98n. 26, 98n. 32
Forrester, V. 11
Fraijó, M. 100n. 41
Fraisse, G. 97n. 18
Frankenstein, V. 47
Frápolli, M. J. 98n. 27
Fukuyama, F., 41

Gadamer, H. G., 97n. 25, 113
Galeotti, A. E. 94n. 2

122   INDEX

Garzón Valdés, E. 96n. 13
Geertz, C. 94n. 5
Gelli, G. B. 6
Giddens, A. 28n. 1
Giner, S. 55n. 6
Gómez, A. 55n. 6
Greisch, J. 29n. 14

Harvey, D. 29n. 5
Havel, V. 13
Hegel, G. W. F. 15, 75, 94n. 4
Herkovits, M. 94n. 5
Herr, D. 29n. 8
Hobbes, T. 118n. 4
Horkheimer, M. 39, 117
Höss, R. 19
Huntington, S. 96n. 12

Jonas, H. 22-4, 26-7, 29n. 8, 29n. 14, 56n. 11

Kafka, F. 104, 109, 114–15
Kant, I. 90, 95n. 10
Klee, P. 109
Kripke, S. 100n. 39
Kroeber, A. L. 94n. 5

La Bruyère, J. de 77
Las Casas, B. de 76
Levi, P. 52-4
Lévinas, E. 100n. 42
Lévi-Strauss, C. 75-6
Lipovetsky, G. 56n. 11
Llull, R. 108
Locke, J. 79-80
Lukacs, G. 64
Lyotard, J.-F. 107

MacIntyre, A. 119n. 4
Manetti, G. 6
Mannheim, K. 105
Marqués, G. L. 99n. 32
Marramao, G. 3

Marx, K. 11, 41, 45, 65, 70-1, 92-3, 116
Menéndez, F. 57n. 24
Mengele, J. 19, 47
Merton, R. 85, 98n. 31
Montaigne, M. de 76, 95n. 11
Montesquieu 78
Moya, C. 33, 36, 55n. 2
Musil, R. 115

Nagel, T. 81, 86, 97n. 21, 97n. 22, 99n. 33
Naishtat, F. 56n. 14, 56n. 16
Nicholson, L. 100n. 40
Nicolás, J. A. 98n. 27
Nietzsche, F. 28n. 3, 108, 111

Olivé, L. 101n. 43
Ortega y Gasset, J. 19, 57n. 21

Parfit, D. 20
Paz, O. 95n. 6, 118
Pico de la Mirandola, G. 6
Popper, K. 64
Proust, M. 109, 114
Putnam, H, 98n. 29, 99n. 35, 99n. 37

Quintanilla, M. A. 99n. 37

Rawls, J. 81
Rella, F. 112
Renaut, A. 16
Ricoeur, P. 69, 89, 94
Riechmann, J. 101n. 44
Riesman, D. 15
Rodríguez Aramayo, R. 95n. 10

Sacristán, M. 27
Sánchez Durá, N. 100n. 38
Sanfélix, V. 100n. 38
Sartre, J. P. 90
Schmitt, C. 56n. 15
Scholem, G. 118
Sennet, R. 15
Sisyphus 48

Spinoza, B. 79
Stuart Mill, J. 11

Taylor, C. 101n. 46
Todorov, T. 78, 95n. 6, 95n. 11

Unamuno, M. de 57n. 21
United Nations 5

Vattimo, G. 40, 55n. 8, 106
Veca, S. 96n. 15
Vespucci, A. 93
Villoro, L. 13
Virilio, P. 94n. 1

Vives, L. 6
Voltaire, 76, 80, 95n. 10

Walzer, M. 82
Weber, M. 21, 56n. 12, 105
Weil, S. 115
Wittgenstein, L. 39, 44, 87-8, 98n. 28, 99n. 35, 100n. 38, 100n. 39, 107, 109
Wizenman, T. 117
Wright, G. H. von 98n. 28

Yourcenar, M. 117

Zarathustra, 112